DAVE & ORPHA BLANCHAT

GOD SHOTS

10 KEYS TO RESTORE YOUR HOPE & EXPERIENCE GOD'S MIRACULOUS POWER IN YOUR LIFE

NASHVILLE

NEW YORK • LONDON • MELBOURNE • VANCOUVER

God Shots

10 Keys to Restore Your Hope and Experience God's Miraculous Power In Your Life

Published in New York, New York, by Morgan James Publishing. Morgan James is a trademark of Morgan James, LLC. www.MorganJamesPublishing.com

Proudly distributed by Publishers Group West®

All Scripture quotations, unless otherwise indicated, are taken from the Holy Bible, New International Version®, NIV®. Copyright ©1973, 1978, 1984, 2011 by Biblica, Inc.™ Used by permission of Zondervan. All rights reserved worldwide. www.zondervan.comThe "NIV" and "New International Version" are trademarks registered in the United States Patent and Trademark Office by Biblica, Inc.™

Morgan James BOGO™

A **FREE** ebook edition is available for you or a friend with the purchase of this print book.

CLEARLY SIGN YOUR NAME ABOVE

Instructions to claim your free ebook edition:
1. Visit MorganJamesBOGO.com
2. Sign your name CLEARLY in the space above
3. Complete the form and submit a photo of this entire page
4. You or your friend can download the ebook to your preferred device

ISBN 9781636982564 paperback
ISBN 9781636982571 ebook
Library of Congress Control Number: 2023940544

Cover & Interior Design by:
Christopher Kirk
www.GFSstudio.com

Morgan James is a proud partner of Habitat for Humanity Peninsula and Greater Williamsburg. Partners in building since 2006.

Get involved today! Visit: www.morgan-james-publishing.com/giving-back

DEDICATION

God Shots *is dedicated to our two amazing children,*
Paige and David.
I do not dare think about my long recovery
without their love and support.
You have endured all of life's changes in stride. Thank you.

I also dedicate this book to my wife Orpha of more than thirty years.
You never gave up on me, either after the accident and before,
when I had given you so many reasons to.
You have loved me through the good and bad,
and in sickness and health.
Thank you, Dear. I love you. Mah!

CONTENTS

INTRODUCTION

"Not only so, but we also glory in our sufferings, because we know that suffering produces perseverance; perseverance, character; and character hope."

— Romans 5:3-4

One of the most beloved films of all time is Frank Capra's *It's a Wonderful Life*. Jimmy Stewart plays George Bailey, a local banker who always wanted to escape his life in the small town of Bedford Falls. While all his classmates were off living exciting lives, he stayed stuck in his humdrum life. George believes his life is a failure because he never accomplished big things.

If you had told me in May of 2014 that these Bible verses would not only become the guiding light of my life but would also be carved on a cane I would use as I learned to walk again, I would have said you were nuts.

Little did I know that the very next month, my life would change forever. I was hit by a semi-tractor and tanker trailer in an accident that broke my body and demolished my own truck beyond recognition. Even more, it shattered my preconceived notions of what God can do in a person's life when we have no choice but to rely totally on His miraculous healing.

As you'll read in the following pages, I barely made it through. In the hours and days after that horrific accident, my life hung in the balance. My wife, Orpha, and my children didn't know if I would survive. The ER staff at Kern Medical Center in Bakersfield, California, even left my contact lenses in because they didn't think I would make it!

But God has a habit of showing up in the most unexpected ways.

As I pulled through a thirty-day coma, nearly two more months of hospital stays, and more than another year at the Centre for Neuro Skills, we saw God work miracles time and again. We started calling them "God Shots." These are the moments when God makes His presence and power known in unmistakable ways.

God Shots were not unique to us. Throughout history, God has shown up in surprising ways for His people. One of the most fascinating examples is from the book of Exodus. Moses asks God what will distinguish him and the Israelites from all the other people on earth. Then he asks God to show him His glory.

Here is God's response:

"And the Lord said, "I will cause all my goodness to pass in front of you, and I will proclaim my name, the Lord, in your presence. I will have mercy on whom I will have mercy, and I will have compassion on whom I will have compassion. But," he said, "you cannot see my face, for no one may see me and live."

Then the Lord said, "There is a place near me where you may stand on a rock. When my glory passes by, I will put you in a cleft in the rock and cover you with my hand until I have passed by. Then I will remove my hand and you will see my back; but my face must not be seen." (Exodus 33:19-23)

It is interesting to note that the Hebrew term for "back" here doesn't mean God's back in a literal sense. It is more the idea that as God passed by and revealed Himself, Moses would see the traces He left behind.

God is still leaving traces today. Throughout my accident and its aftermath, and in a thousand ways since then, we have seen God Shots—traces He has left behind to make Himself known. There is another word we use for these traces—*miracles*.

What is a miracle? A miracle, to me, is the result of things that can only be created by divine inspiration, by God Himself. Miracles are events that go beyond mere coincidence or happenstance.

Do miracles still happen today? The world would have you believe that there are no miracles, just good luck and bad luck—just western medicine, mandates, and exact science. In the following pages, I will present a case that should prove beyond a reasonable doubt that yes, there are miracles, and yes, I have witnessed them in my own life. And that, yes, if you look through the correct lens, you have seen them, experienced them, or know of them, too.

These miracles, or God Shots, can lead us to crossroads or intersections where our choice determines the outcome, where free will provides us with the route to be taken and the impact to be made. My initial intersection, the accident, was not my choice. No. But my reaction to it, the actions I took after the accident at that intersection, were mine to choose.

Much of life is how we react to what happens to us. Free will allows us to choose. There are only a limited number of "have to's" in this life. We have to live. We have to die. And we have to pay taxes. The rest is pretty much up to us and God!

You'll hear more of my story in the following pages. But this book is not just about my story. I'm here to give you hope as you face your own troubles, dilemmas, and life-threatening situations.

As a man or woman, you may think you have it all figured out, but you need God's wisdom and healing power in your life. That's why I wrote this book—to tell the truth not only about my story but your story as well. We may be very different, and you may not have gone through a horrible automobile accident. But no matter who you are, where you're from, or what you've been through, I know two things about you:

1. You have trauma and pain of your own.
2. You need the healing power of God in your life.

This book is my story of experiencing a horrible accident, seeing God move in astounding ways, and what I have learned since then. I would never wish an accident on anyone, but I can tell you today that I am a different person—a better person—because of the accident. When you picked up this book, your first inclination was probably not to read a book about an accident. But sometimes, it takes going through the darkness to lead us to the light.

You may feel strong. You may think you have it all together. You may believe that nothing like a horrible auto accident can happen to you. But there comes a time in every person's life when they must admit they need the healing power of God in their own life.

But it's not just about your life. It's also about your spouse, kids, family, coworkers, and everyone else whose lives you touch. Like the ripples from a pebble tossed into a still pool, our lives go forward, touching countless others. We have a responsibility to fulfill our potential as men and women. I hope it doesn't take a life-threatening accident for you to fully rely on God.

This book is organized into two parts. In Part 1, you will hear the story of my accident and all the God Shots we have seen since that day. Even through a coma, two extended hospital stays, and rehabilitation and recovery that continues to this day, God has been faithful. It is a true story of hope and restoration.

Part 2 focuses on helping you experience God Shots in your own life. We will explore ten keys to success based on what I learned about life, leadership, and more.

This is the book's main message: Don't wait until an accident or other tragedy to change your life. Take charge of your life and let God work in every area so you can be the man or woman He has called you to be.

As you read, you will notice that my wife, Orpha, plays a big part in this story. In fact, she plays such a big part that she needed to be the co-author! In Part 1, we each offer our perspectives on the accident and its aftermath. In Part 2, she weighs in by sharing her thoughts from time to time.

I would not have made it through without her love and support. After the accident, I was in a coma for thirty days, so I don't remember anything from that time or even that week. She has been vital in recalling the details of events. Orpha often says we are "created on purpose for a purpose." She used this Les Brown quote to remind me of this truth again and again as she stuck by my side and encouraged me not to give up on God's purpose for my life.

God can redeem our pain and suffering. As Romans 5:3-4 tells us, suffering results in perseverance, character, and hope. When the Apostle Paul wrote to the believers in Rome nearly two thousand years ago, he was trying to help them understand how God can use suffering for God. As you read my story and what I have learned over the last seven years, I pray that you will experience that as well.

God saved me from the horrific accident in June 2014. For what, I'm not sure. But I know this; the harvest is plentiful, and the workers are few. Therefore, I ask the Lord of the harvest to use me as He sees fit!

I pray the same thing for you as well. I ask to help you become a vessel for miracles in your own life and an instrument for miracles in the lives of others, including your family and friends. I encourage you to do whatever is necessary to open yourself up to the possibility of being Christ's hands and feet for His Kingdom.

Thank you for taking this journey with us. You can learn more about us at god-shots.com and on Instagram at godshots_ourstory.

~Dave

Part 1

OUR STORY OF HOPE & RESTORATION

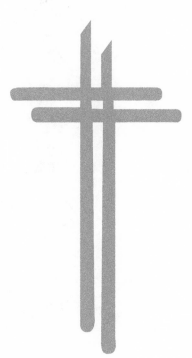

Chapter 1

THE ACCIDENT

BY DAVE

I t's funny how so much of our lives are on autopilot. We get up in the morning, have breakfast, say goodbye to the family, spend a day at work, drive home, have dinner, watch a little TV, then go to bed. Rinse and repeat for about thirty years, and there, you have a typical American life.

I can't say mine was much different. As the VP of Operations for Paramount Farms (Wonderful Pistachios and Almonds) in California's San Joaquin Valley, I took great satisfaction in my work. I had the privilege of finding and developing leaders and doing work that was mostly fulfilling. We produced private label and Wonderful Pistachios and Almonds, a popular brand shipped around the world and loved by millions.

But I'd be lying if I said that life hadn't gotten a little comfortable. You might have even called it routine. As I climbed into my truck at the end of the workday on June 24, 2014, I had no idea that my routine was about to change drastically.

I headed home on my usual route, going south on Highway 33 near Bakersfield, California. I had driven that route over 5,000 times in my twenty years at Paramount and was looking forward to the weekend we had planned to vacation in Idaho.

I'm a detail person, so I always try to be aware of my surroundings, especially when driving. As I came upon the intersection of Highway 33 and Highway 46, I probably took note of a pistachio semi-truck with attached trailers going westbound and turning into the northbound lane of Highway 33. However, I didn't see the semi with a tanker trailer full of oil on the other side that was going straight and was about to run a red light.

I don't remember anything about the collision, but I can't imagine the noise it must have made. The shattering of glass, the crumbling of steel, and the impact! My world went black as my truck and body gave way to the semi colliding with me. Everything changed in an instant.

However, I was not the only Blanchat family member whose life was about to be turned upside down.

* * *

BY ORPHA

I was going about my day when I received a call from Curtis, a long-time friend of ours and the Vice President of IT at Wonderful. "Hello, Orpha. Has anyone called you yet?"

"No, what's up?"

"Orpha, David's been in a terrible car accident!" David was coming home from work and had a green light at an intersection, but the semi had a red light. The semi hit David, going sixty miles an hour. It was catastrophic. Curtis relayed to Orpha that Abe was only a mile from work at the Highway 33 and 46 Texaco getting himself and his intern snacks and sodas to help them work a bit longer, making reports David would need the next day. Abe was a good friend of the family and one of the employees at Wonderful. Curtis gave me Abe's phone number, so I frantically dialed it!

"This is Abe."

"Abe, this is Orpha. How is he? What's going on?"

"He has a pulse, he's unconscious, and there's a lot of blood. Dave just got here, and Orpha, he's broken." One of the most significant God Shots was Abe! I'll let Dave tell you that later. Then Abe handed the phone to Dave Szeflin, the Executive VP who functioned as the organization's President.

"Dave, this is Orpha. What's going on?" I could hear men in the background yelling and what seemed like crying. I knew it was bad. Dave gave me a run-down of the status, minus details I did not need to hear.

I said, "Dave, I want you to pray with him audibly. Let him know Jesus is with him, and he'll be okay." He did so, and I could hear an "Amen" from everyone there.

Dave continued the update. "Life Flight is en route, and he'll be going to KMC." Kern Medical Center was a twenty-minute flight from the scene of the accident. Talk about a God shot! We were so fortunate Abe had come upon Dave at the scene soon after the accident. He had phoned Dave Szeflin, who immediately called the nurse at Paramount. She had set the Medivac helicopter in motion.

"I'm on my way to KMC," I said.

I hung up and desperately tried to do the next tasks. I was struggling to make phone calls. My emotions were swirling, and nothing seemed to work. *When was the last time I talked to David? Why? Please, Lord!*

But I managed to pull myself together enough to post on Facebook, "Dave's been in an accident, please pray," and then made sure our four-year-old, David, and daughter, Paige, knew Dave was hurt but going to be okay. When Pastor James Lair, our Pastor at First Assembly of God, heard about the accident, he immediately came to the house to help me navigate phone calls and calm my spirit. My dear friend, Michelle, came over without being called and picked up David. Then my friend Taryn came over to take me to the hospital because there was no way I could drive myself.

* * *

BY DAVE

Back at the scene of the accident, others had arrived to help. It just so happened that a group of respiratory therapists were at the stoplight on the other side of the road when the semi hit me. When they saw the accident, they drove over and began to clear my airway.

Several firefighters from the Lost Hills Fire Department came almost immediately. They often worked out at our company's gym facilities. When they heard about the accident, they came immediately.

One of them, Gregg McGill, had befriended Ryan Barton, an employee of mine at the time. Ryan texted Gregg, *Did you run a call out here?* Ryan told him my condition. *Still alive!* After the accident, Ryan continued to send Gregg regular updates on me.

We were fortunate to have not just one but three fire departments in the San Joaquin Valley arrive on the scene that day: Buttonwillow, McKittrick, and Lost Hills. We will be eternally grateful for their help.

When Gregg arrived, he spotted my truck and the semi on its side about a hundred yards west of my truck on the highway. His captain said, "Gregg, you check the pickup."

A civilian, most likely Abe, said, "That's the number two guy at Paramount!" But to an EMT like Gregg, that's not important! He later said to me, "We treat everyone the same, from the president to a field worker!"

Gregg tried my pickup's driver door, but it was stuck shut. Then he asked the crew's engineer, along with the available civilians, to grab the extrication equipment. The door popped open fairly easily, and he left the extrication equipment in place to keep it open because it kept wanting to spring closed.

Then Gregg popped into the back seat to put me on oxygen, install a C-collar, and cut my seatbelt off. He had to bear-hug me to get me out of the crumpled vehicle. He later said the civilians were amazing!

Whenever EMTs work with a person they suspect has brain injuries, they use something called the Glasgow Coma Scale (GCS) to determine their level of consciousness. The scale goes from 1-15. A score of 13-15 is mild, 9-12 is moderate, 3-8 is severe, and a 1 or 2 means you are close to dead! I tested as a 3 at first, but after getting me out of the truck, Gregg was able to get a response from rubbing my sternum. He then upgraded me to a 4, a slight improvement, but I was still in the severe range. Gregg told me later that he thought to himself, *This guy doesn't have a chance.*

After I was safely aboard the Medivac, Gregg ran to the semi that had crashed into me. It was lying on its side. As soon as he arrived, the captain took one look at him and said, "You're done!" He then realized he was covered in blood . . . my blood!

Later, Gregg remembers getting a call from the lady who cleans his gear and gets it ready. "What did you *do*!?" she asked. She had to wash his outfit twice to get it clean.

I had lost a lot of blood, and there was no guarantee I would make it. With me in the air and Orpha on the highway, both racing to the hospital from different directions, time was not on our side.

But thanks to Dave Szelfin's prayer, I was not alone.

Chapter 2

MINUTE BY MINUTE

BY DAVE

When you experience something as traumatic as a massive car accident, every second counts. If you have a traumatic brain injury, it's vital to get to the hospital and be stabilized within an hour or less. Otherwise, you probably won't survive.

The medical community calls it the "golden hour." Thanks to Dave Szeflin making the call, I was on the Life Flight helicopter to KMC (Kern Medical Center in Bakersfield, CA) and made it to the ER within that crucial first hour.

You are given a code name when you're admitted to the ER. My name at KMC was Romeo. Later, Taryn made a t-shirt with "Team Romeo" printed on the front with Philippians 4:13 on the back. "I can do all things through him who gives me strength." That's a perfect reminder of how we were relying on God and His people for strength, especially in these first critical hours.

Once I got to the hospital, they were able to assess my injuries. I was a broken man who was "tore up from the floor up." I sustained injuries that still affect me to this day. My right ankle was crushed. I still can't move it. All I can feel is pain in my right foot, but otherwise, it's numb. Both lower legs and feet suffer from neuropathy, which makes me feel like someone's putting cigarettes out on them, 24-7! I take hydrocodone and gabapentin to make it bearable. My left hand and arm are partially paralyzed and numb. My spleen has been removed. I had a feeding tube in for what seemed like forever.

My left eye was damaged, and I saw double until surgery on my eye muscles corrected some of it. My eyes bounced up and down rapidly (a condition called "saccade"). I still see double when I look to my left, but I don't have to put tape on my glasses anymore or close one eye all the time.

The hit on my left side made my face look like a bear had mauled me! My left arm was all cut up and full of glass shards. We were still removing glass for months afterward. My left shoulder and all my left ribs were broken. My left lung was punctured and deflated. Both my neck and back had broken vertebrae.

And then, there was the DAI (Diffuse Axonal Injury), a type of traumatic brain injury. It has been described as resembling the effects of "shaken baby syndrome." DIA occurs when the brain quickly shifts inside the skull and experiences trauma. When that happens, the "axons" (long connecting fibers in the brain) are broken off. It caused me to lose my memory.

In addition, blood vessels in and around my brain were damaged or severed. That cut the flow of nutrients and oxygen off to brain tissues, leading to the death of parts of my brain. For the first several days, doctors would show my wife the new "flowering" areas of my brain where bleeds were occurring or finally being seen through Computed Tomography (CT) scans or Magnetic Resonance Imaging (MRI). Much of the brain was affected. The frontal lobe, which is responsible for, among other things, language and executive functions, was damaged. The temporal lobe that contains memory was affected. Delivering this news usually fell to a neurologist my wife and others nicknamed Dr. Giggles. It felt like He *never* had a positive or kind word for Orpha!

Months later, after I'd left Rancho Los Amigos (the rehabilitation hospital), I returned to KMC with Orpha to thank the UCI nurses, physician assistants, and the head of surgery. And, of course, to finally meet Dr. Giggles. That day just so happened to be his last day at KMC before going into private practice. We got a room, and Dr. Giggles was summoned. He arrived minutes later, looked at Orpha, looked at me, then looked back to Orpha with a sense of slight recognition. I said, "Ta Da!" His only comment was, "If I hadn't seen you for myself . . ." He shook his head, then shook my hand.

It's unbelievable that 90% of patients with my level of damage never wake up. The vast majority of the other 10% who wake up are put into nursing homes and die there. Thankfully, thousands around the world were praying for me. In addition, Orpha had read that fish oil is good for those who suffer brain damage and are in a coma. She asked the ER staff to give me some, and they said it had to go through their pharmacy. As far as they were concerned, there was no proof, and it wasn't part of their protocol. The head of surgery came in and made sure they gave me fish oil through my feeding tube. As far as I know, it's been an option for patients ever since.

I stayed in a coma for thirty days. During that time, Orpha always wanted someone in the room with me in case I woke up. She didn't want to leave me alone. She made a schedule that always put at least one person in the room with me. It was no small feat since I was at

KMC for forty days and Rancho Los Amigos for another forty days. If there were two people together on the schedule, she would try to pair a solid believer with a non-believer or someone with different views. It created quite the opportunity to educate and evangelize during that terrible time.

The non-believers and newer believers had so many questions. They would ask things like, "Can you explain this part of the Bible I don't understand?" or "What are these b-attitudes about?" Some people had their faith strengthened, others heard about Christ for the first time, and some were even saved.

That was Romans chapter 5 in action. God was using Orpha to bless others and introduce them to Jesus amid a horrible situation. The only reason she was able to do that was because of her deep faith. I may have been the one in the hospital bed, but she was right there beside me, being the hands and feet of Jesus to me every step of the way.

* * *

BY ORPHA

I'm so glad that Taryn, my best friend, drove me to the hospital because I would not have been able to think about the road or the traffic. All you can think about are the questions that flood everyone's mind in that situation. *Why did this happen to us? Are they going to recover? Is our family going to be okay? Seriously, haven't we been through enough?*

I had no idea if Dave was going to live or die. I was in shock and disbelief. Above all, I was terrified of what I might discover when I got to the hospital.

When I arrived at KMC, I walked into the ER and found the intake nurse. I said, "I'm here to find out about Dave Blanchat."

She looked at her computer and said, "I can tell you we have a pulse." Then I waited for what seemed like hours. Finally, the head doctor of the trauma unit came out and asked, "Who's here for David?"

Several people raised their hands, and she said, "No, who's the spouse?"

I spoke up and said, "I'm his spouse." I approached her, and she began to explain.

"Well, he's critical, critical, critical."

I said, "I know what critical is, but what do you mean by 'critical, critical, critical'?"

She said, "I mean that it's minute by minute, whether he lives or dies. I could go back in there, and he could be dead." It's hard to fault a doctor for being so blunt because they see trauma and death every day. It's not *their* loved one they are talking about. But it was clear she didn't expect Dave to survive.

They never even took out his contacts. They also didn't take off his wedding ring, which they do when they think the patient will be in the hospital for a long time. It was a day or two later when I had to ask them to take out his contacts.

They thought he was a dead man. But God isn't in the business of giving up. As the days went on, it was clear God was intervening. Those "God Shots" were coming on a regular basis.

For example, when Dave first went into the ER, they told me his hand, wrist, elbow, and shoulder were all broken. Then a day or two later, they came back and said they were actually not broken.

I couldn't figure out if God had healed those parts of his body or if they were misdiagnosed to begin with. These are professionals we're talking about. They are in the business of diagnosing broken bones and identifying all sorts of physical problems. So, for them to come back a short time later and tell us they were not broken . . . I can only assume God miraculously healed Dave in that short time because so many were praying for him—for us.

I also believe it was a God Shot that Dave was in spectacular physical shape. He had been going to the gym a lot and planned to run a marathon soon. There was one point in the ER when Dave's blood pressure dropped to 43, and the doctors went crazy. They told me, "You need to call his regular doctor and let us know what his resting heart rate is."

I finally got in touch with his doctor, who was on the golf course. He said, "Yes, that's his resting heart rate. He's in amazing shape." That was not news to us because we had both just been to the doctor for our yearly checkups. In his notes, the doctor had written, "If all the men David's age were in this shape, I'd have no patients." That's how much in shape he was.

I saw God respond in these moments, even from that first night in the ICU. I couldn't see what was ahead, but I knew it would be hard. There would be a lot of unknowns. But a few days later, our four-year-old son, David, expressed a simple faith and urgency we all felt. He said, "Just have Dad rub some dirt in it and get home already." It was a running joke in our family, and the much-needed humor came as a welcome gift.

Time and again throughout this ordeal, we saw God do amazing things in Dave's recovery. We knew He would be with us on the mountaintop as well as in the valley.

Thankfully, we didn't have to walk the valley alone, thanks to some dear friends who came to walk beside us.

Chapter 3

FRIENDS IN HIGH PLACES

BY ORPHA

A hospital can be a lonely and frightening place. Even under the best circumstances, you are in a place full of brokenness and tragedy. But when surrounded by people who love you, a hospital can transform into a place of blessing and hope.

I can't imagine going through our ordeal without the love and support of a vast network of friends. Every day of the forty days we were at KMC, ten or twelve people waited in line in the hallway to see Dave. It was like a revolving door. I'd say, "Okay, John, you go in. And when you come back out, let Taryn go in."

I loved it because it took the pressure off me to some degree. Some days, I would only see Dave for an hour because so many people came to see him.

The hospital was very good about all this. They let one person stay with him at all times. We didn't even have to leave during a shift change, which is uncommon when you're in the ICU. But we were very respectful.

People would come and pray over Dave. They would also sing over him. Our friend, Don Jacobson, came in and played the saxophone. Others would come and anoint him with oil. Those things happened daily. I was never by myself in the ICU. At times, it was just me and my friend, Diane, because it was 7:00 a.m. or later in the afternoon.

Diane was a Godsend. She is a teacher as well as a tutor in the summertime. Typically, she tutors four or five different kids in the summer. She had been at the hospital every day for a couple of weeks when I asked, "Diane, why aren't you tutoring?"

She said, "It's the weirdest thing. I don't have any kids to tutor this summer." That was a real God Shot because that allowed Diane to be there with me every day. The day before Dave got out of the hospital, she came to me and said, "I'm so sorry. I've got a student." The timing of it couldn't have been more perfect.

The thing I love about Diane is that we have the same stoic type of personality. I'm not a drama person, and neither is she. Sometimes we wouldn't even talk to each other. We would sit there in the room, each doing our own thing. Her presence was all I needed. It was a real blessing because it was so helpful, having another person who was a rock—who had a level head.

Diane was with me in the daytime, but in the late afternoons, more people would begin to show up. Our friends, Sharon and Randy, made sure I ate every day. Others came during their lunch hour or on the weekends. Another constant was Dave's mom, who came from Washington state and stayed the duration of his hospital stays. She was a tremendous help.

The ICU closed at 10:00 p.m., and they had to kick us out. We just went downstairs and waited in the lobby. Even then, people were still filing in one after another. Even though Dave was in a coma, he was still experiencing a sleep cycle. They would say, "Okay, now bring in just two people," and those two would spend the night with him. He was never alone the whole time because people had rotating shifts. One of the people Dave supervised at work set up a schedule, so there was a rotation of guys from Wonderful who stayed with him.

The main thing was that I didn't want him to wake up from his coma alone. How incredibly frightening that would be! Imagine waking up in a hospital bed with all the tubes, wires, and machines, then having a nurse walk in and explain what happened.

To prevent that from happening, everyone had a script. If Dave woke up, they were to say, "You were in a car accident. You were by yourself. You're going to be okay."

Later, when Dave began to wake up from the coma, we had ten more days in the hospital before we transferred to the rehabilitation center. In those moments when he would wake up, we could see the fear in his eyes, and someone would reassure him and say, "It's okay; you were in a car accident. The kids were not with you. You're going to be okay."

I didn't want that to come from a nurse. I wanted it to come from a friend or family member.

The Blanchat family made up a big part of the people who visited Dave and stayed with him in the ICU, but there were many others. I didn't know all of them. Dave was in AA for a time, and I didn't know the people from that part of his world.

I remember one guy who walked in, covered from head to toe with tattoos. There was a lot of gang activity in our area, so I didn't think anything of it. He looked around the waiting room for a bit, then finally walked over to our group and said, "Is Orpha here?"

I said, "Yes, that's me."

He said, "Hi, I'm Rich, and I'm here to see Dave." He was only one of many people I had never met before, but they knew Dave and were coming to see him.

Another notable visitor was a gentleman who came in looking like a bum. I thought, *Who is this guy?* It turned out he was an undercover detective working out of LA. I had no idea Dave knew this guy.

This may sound strange, but I had no idea Dave had so many people who loved him. Of course, I loved him, and so did our families. But I was overwhelmed by the people who kept coming out of the woodwork to show their love and support.

But it wasn't just the support at the hospital; it was the support at home as well. One of the many God Shots we experienced during that time was how He provided care for our kids. Our babysitter, Natalie, was an absolute blessing, as was our church family. Church members brought food for the kids every day for nearly three months after the accident. Friends always made sure they got to school and church. What a huge blessing. They were the same wonderful people who brought us food for thirty days after Sarah Anne passed away. (I'll share more about Sarah Anne later in the book.)

I read somewhere once that it is important to be part of something bigger than just you and your immediate family. Our church family and circle of friends were a living reminder of that truth. They practiced what Romans 12:4-5 teaches us. "For just as each of us has one body with many members, and these members do not all have the same function, so in Christ we, though many, form one body, and each member belongs to all the others." We are always better together than we are alone.

* * *

Dave wasn't alone at Rancho Los Amigos, the rehabilitation center, after he transferred there. People made the two-hour drive every day to sit with him.

My brother, Orval, was also there the whole time. He was gone so much he almost got fired from his job. He told his employer, "You don't understand. My brother-in-law can't wake up alone, and I have to be there." Orval was always questioning the doctors' care. He was constantly Googling their diagnoses and even noticed a few things that could be done differently. It was a love/hate relationship between him and the doctors. They told him to quit Googling everything. And that's how he got the nickname "Dr. Google."

I was there during the day, and other people would be there at night. They made sure to always shave his goatee for him. Abe came and shaved his goatee many days of the week. The amount of love people showered upon our family was amazing.

We did our best to boost Dave's faith during his coma, even though he couldn't hear us. I asked people to read to Dave from the Bible each night in addition to the devotional *Streams in the Desert*. But we also had friends who were atheists, Sikhs, and Muslims. I paired them up with Christian believers to make sure they were exposed to the Christian faith. So, in an unexpected way, the accident became an opportunity to share our faith with nonbelievers. We were always working for God's kingdom.

Dave also had friends who came in and teased him. "Dave, if you don't wake up, we're going to paint your toenails! We're going to give you a tattoo!" They really harassed him while he was in a coma, all in a good-natured way, of course.

That was a difficult time for us, but it was also beautiful. The love that our family, friends, and co-workers showed to Dave was overwhelming. And he deserved it. He's a good man. It would have been easier for Dave to just die. But because of their love, he kept fighting and pressing on.

One of Dave's friends made a great observation. "It couldn't have happened to a better person." He was absolutely right. Most people would have crumbled and given up, but not Dave. The love and respect I have for Dave today is far greater than I've ever had because I've watched him overcome one of the most challenging things people could ever go through.

He had to relearn so many things. In essence, he became a new person. But he did so in a powerful way and became closer to God because of it. Both of us appreciate life so much more these days. We don't take anything for granted, and we take every challenge as it comes.

Ironically, one of the challenges we had to face was figuring out how to deal with the family of the man who put Dave in the hospital in the first place.

* * *

Jesus once said, "'You have heard that it was said, 'Love your neighbor and hate your enemy.' But I tell you, love your enemies and pray for those who persecute you, that you may be children of your Father in heaven.'" (Matthew 5:43-45a). While it may not seem like you encounter enemies every day, you do have to face people on occasion who have caused you a lot of harm.

That was the case in the hospital soon after Dave was admitted. We learned that the man who hit him, who had caused us so much pain and grief, was also at KMC. How do you respond to that kind of person? How do you put Jesus's words into action when everything within you wants to strike out in anger? Those were some of the questions and emotions I faced, particularly within those first few days after the accident.

From the first day Dave was in the hospital, people were always bringing us food. We had a constant stream of snacks, sandwiches, drinks, and everything you could imagine. So, we had an abundance of riches when it came to food and refreshments. One night as I was in the ICU waiting room with a few of my dearest friends, we noticed a small Hispanic woman pacing back and forth and looking very distraught. She looked like she could pass out at any moment; her legs kept buckling. I knew she needed prayer. I remember looking at my friends, all prayer warriors, wondering why none of them had noticed her need. Then I heard from God.

I'm not a person who audibly "hears from God" all the time, but I can tell you this; I audibly heard God speaking to me, "If not you, who? If you won't pray for her, who will?"

I walked over to her and realized she didn't speak much English, but fortunately, prayer does not need to be interpreted. It is a universal language, and she knew I was praying for her. After that, I sat her down and offered her food, and she accepted. I was still confused about why it had to be me. Then a few days later, we found out why. She was the wife of the man who hit Dave. If not me, then who?

We eventually learned that when this man hit Dave, his semi-truck flipped. He sustained a broken back and neck, which caused him to become quadriplegic, along with several other serious injuries. We also got the full story of what happened. The day before the accident, he had gone home and stayed up almost all night watching World Cup soccer. He drove his truck the next day with almost no sleep. It was irresponsible for him to drive without having a full night's rest or at least broken his trip into sections.

He didn't set out to hit Dave or cause so much trouble. He was simply trying to put food on the table and provide for his family. He was a soccer fan who stayed up too late and paid a dear price for it. He had no intention of causing so much harm to his family or ours.

Because I had the opportunity to pray with his wife before I knew who she was, seeing her as fragile as I was, I held no animosity towards her or her husband. I had the opportunity to break bread with her and her family many times during both hospital stays.

Chapter 4

THE AWAKENING

BY ORPHA

Rooms in the intensive care unit at KMC are different than regular hospital rooms. The front-facing walls of the rooms are all glass so the nurses can see in, and the doors are sliding glass doors. I had gotten used to this, so when something looked different, I noticed.

One day, I went in to see Dave and heard a ruckus coming from his room. The glass doors were closed, and I could see Dave's father, Richard, and his dear friend, Lance, yelling at him. Debbie, Dave's Physician's Assistant, said, "We've passed the thirty-day mark, and this needs to be over. A person can't stay in a coma for thirty days or more. They get too comfortable being asleep. It's no good. He needs this, and you've got to wake him up."

So, they started applying pressure to Dave's sternum and rubbing it. They were pinching him and yelling at him. "Come on, Dave, you need to wake up. You can't do this. This is the time for you to wake up!" Debbie later told us that she felt Richard and Lance saved Dave because they were relentless in getting him to wake up. The longer a person stays comfortable in their coma, the more difficult it is to wake them up.

Andy, one of Dave's workout partners, was also a big help getting Dave to wake up. Whenever they ran or worked out together, they had these sayings they repeated to each other to spur them on. Andy would go into Dave's room and chant those phrases—sometimes loudly! He also worked with Dave by moving his legs back and forth and pumping his arms.

In the ICU, we always had music playing. There was a lot of laughing and joking. An ICU is normally a somber place, so this was completely out of character for a typical hospital setting—especially in a room where the patient is in a coma. We also had people come in to anoint Dave and sing over him. I will always be grateful to my nieces and nephew for singing to Dave in the ICU. What a beautiful time. During those days, we formed some of the biggest bonds with friends and family in the ICU, where we kept the atmosphere light and cheerful.

Dave also had "Get Well Soon" signs and pictures posted all over the room. The whole place was covered in signs, pictures, and posters—even the ceiling. The hospital staff had never seen that before.

Dave started coming around, slowly awakening. Then he would slip back into sleep. In real life, coming out of a coma doesn't happen like in the movies, where a person suddenly throws open their eyes and is wide awake. Over a matter of days, Dave came around.

Debbie said what helped Dave overcome was the love, the prayers, the joking, and the antics that went on in his room. That is what saved him. But the most important part was the prayers.

* * *

BY DAVE

When you start to come out of a coma, the first part is called the "awakening." You're not totally coherent, but you're starting to emerge from a state of being unconscious. I don't even remember the first time I woke up. I'm not even sure that "waking up" is the right term because I would have my eyes open for a little while, then would drift back asleep.

Every time I woke up, it was like it was the first time. I was so confused. Was anyone else with me in the accident? Were my kids okay? So, someone would have to review what had happened. "You were in a truck by yourself and got into an accident. Your kids are fine." Our daughter, Paige, and our babysitter, Natalie, put together a photo album of my life, and they had to go over it every time. "Here's your wife, here are your kids," and so on. They had to do that every time I woke up so I wouldn't get confused. (Natalie is like a daughter to us. She stayed with the kids the entire time I was in the hospital. We often took her on vacations with us.)

When it got to the end of the month, the hospital told my family that if I didn't wake up within the next day or two, I'd have to go into a nursing home because I would probably have no chance of regaining consciousness.

My insurance had already run out. When that happened, Dave Szeflin asked the people at KMC, "Where is the best hospital Dave should be?"

They said, "This one."

And Dave said, "Then he stays here. I will make sure the company covers the bill if the insurance stops paying you guys." The pressure to leave was off. That was around the time I began my real awakening process.

The funny thing is, as I mentioned earlier, I don't remember the accident. Everything I know about the accident and being at KMC was told to me by someone else. I don't even remember the week at work before I was hit.

The only thing I remember from the time around the coma is the dreams. I was at our grandparents' beach cabin in Poulsbo, Washington. It was filling with water. Then I was being picked up by the ambulance from our driveway to take me to Rancho Los Amigos . . . from our driveway! Strange how the mind tries to fill the voids.

I guess that's how our minds respond to trauma. Wherever there's a void, our mind creates stories, sometimes wild and untamed, sometimes bizarre and downright strange. Our minds will do almost anything to avoid telling us the truth.

But my mind had mostly been out of commission for a month. It was time to wake up and begin facing the truth that there was still a long, tough road ahead.

* * *

BY ORPHA

Whenever a loved one is in the hospital facing a life-or-death situation, you are obviously concerned about their well-being. But that is not the only concern that occupies your mind. You are also dealing with the practical reality of a thousand other details to think about—insurance, transportation, money, visitor schedules, potential work issues, and so much more.

One of the many things I thought about in the first week after the accident was Dave's truck. His truck was completely totaled, so I called the insurance company and told them what had happened. They called back and told me how much money they could give me for it.

Just like many people think when they are dealing with insurance companies, I thought to myself, *that number doesn't sound right.*

So, I called a friend of ours, Ryan Nieland, a car broker, and asked for help. Fortunately, he was able to intervene on my behalf with the insurance company. They paid the full value of the truck.

Throughout this whole ordeal, there was always someone around who could help me navigate things I couldn't have done for myself. To me, those were God Shots.

Whenever someone called and asked for papers—attorneys, for example—I would say, "Well, they're in the safe." Dave used to say to me, "Here's the number for the safe," and I would never be concerned about it. He would say, "You need to write this down or have it somewhere." And I would nonchalantly say, "I've got it, don't worry about it." (An important note to wives: know the code to the safe and credit card information. Don't get caught off guard!)

But when it came time to access some papers inside the safe, I did not have the number. I had no idea what the safe code was. I had my friend, Ryan, come over, and we tried for nearly an hour to open the safe. We kept putting in codes, and finally, by the grace of God, we got one that worked.

I always felt like God had my back. If someone asked me for something or wanted me to make a decision and I didn't know how to handle it, God always brought someone into my life I could call on for help.

People of faith always talk about being comforted by God's presence, and that's important. But *how* does God make himself known? How does he help us sense his presence and peace? Through other people.

I was never alone through this whole journey. God made himself known to me through the presence of others who helped me with every aspect of making it through.

But there were also times when I felt God's presence directly. I had to draw on His strength to help others even though I was hurting.

My normal routine was to cry on the way to the hospital, shut the tears off, and walk in. I knew I would have to make hard decisions every day, and doctors would want to talk to me as soon as I walked in. We need to talk about this procedure. We need to do this or that. The doctor's questions never seemed to end, and I couldn't be a weepy wife incapable of making decisions. I had to be the strong one.

But when I left for the day, I could cry all the way home. I would dry my tears off when I got into the house because we had kids at home, and I felt like I had to be strong for everybody. So, I just cried in the car.

I remember one day I was crying in the car; I got angry because I was so strong in the hospital that people would come out of Dave's room and cry to me. I would say, "It's okay. This is not His plan because God said He had a plan not to harm you, but to give you a hope and a future."

I believe that idea, taken from Jeremiah 29:11, with every fiber of my being. So, I prayed with people and reassured them that Dave would be fine. That day as I was driving, I grabbed the steering wheel really hard and started shaking it, screaming, "God, what's wrong with me? Why aren't I more upset? Why am I so even-keeled?"

Other people were freaking out; Dave's family was upset, and there I was, trying to keep a level head and make good decisions. I didn't hear an audible voice, but I could clearly sense God telling me, "This is peace and comfort I give to you. Go." In that moment, a deep sense of peace and comfort came over me. I was reminded of John 16:33, "I have told you these things, so that in me you may have peace. In this world, you will have trouble. But take heart! I have overcome the world."

I knew I would be okay—that I could handle it. And from then on, I didn't spend as much time in tears. But what did God mean by "go"? I felt He was telling me to let people know that I believed Dave would be okay—that this wasn't God's plan.

It bolstered my spirit to know that God's got this. Even if Dave died or was left in a vegetative state, things would be okay. We had already been through so much in our marriage with the loss of our infant daughter due to TD a few years before, his alcohol problem, our resulting separation, and much more.

There was no way God intended for us to end up in a bad place. Because of my conviction and my sense of God's mission for me in this situation, I was able to be super strong in all my decisions. If someone brought me paperwork to put Dave in a nursing home, I could tell them it wasn't going to happen. If they wanted to do a procedure that wasn't aligned with the hope I had, the procedure wasn't going to happen.

God gave me the strength to make those tough decisions. And because of my strength, it gave others confidence when I made them.

It was a good thing, too, because we were getting ready for a whole new set of challenges to get Dave out of the hospital.

We were at KMC for ten more days after Dave came out of his coma, trying to convince his doctor that we needed to put him in rehabilitation. However, they wanted to send him to a nursing home. Their whole attitude was, "He's woken up, but this is it. It's the best you can hope for."

Of course, I was ready to do battle with them; I wasn't going to give up. Especially not after we had come that far. So, the doctor said, "Listen, if you can get him to sit up on his own and flash me an OK sign or a thumbs up, we will send him to rehabilitation."

My brother was there, and he called one of the respiratory thera-pists and said, "We've just got to get him to sit up." So, with his help, my brother got Dave to sit up.

Just then, the doctor poked her head into the room. She scoffed a bit at my brother and said, "Did he sit up by himself?"

Dave gave her a thumbs up, and she said, "All right, let's go. Let's get him out of here tomorrow." It was amazing.

Dave wasn't speaking much yet at that point. KMC is a teaching hospital, and one day around the time Dave had awakened from the coma, as the doctor was walking by with her students, they came into his room and started to do the usual routine where the doctor reviews what is wrong with the patient. She was explaining that Dave had a traumatic brain injury, was in a vegetative state, and so forth.

Suddenly, Dave said, "Hello!"

"What did he just say? Did he just say hello?"

"Yep, hello," Dave said. His recovery was a shock. Even from a medical perspective, they felt that what they saw was impossible.

As a side note, it took about a year after the accident for another doctor to do neuro scans on Dave. They performed a procedure where he had to watch TV, and the scan showed his neurons firing. The doctor came out and said, "I need you to know that his neurons and his pathways are not firing enough for him to be able to sit and have a conversation with me. What I'm seeing should be impossible. Accord-ing to the scan, he should not be able to communicate at this level."

Yet Dave walked in under his own power and had a conversation with the doctor. He truly is a walking miracle. Now, whenever I take him to the doctor, I have to send them a phone book-sized collection of documentation on his injuries, and they are truly amazed that he is able to function at such a high level.

Once Dave was cleared to leave the hospital, we began the process of transferring him to Rancho Los Amigos in Downey, California, to begin the next chapter of his recovery. The day he left the hospital, our friends and family lined the halls, cheering him on. He gave everyone a big thumbs up as he was wheeled into the ambulance to be transported to Rancho Los Amigos. I am forever grateful for all the support and prayer we received. I know without all of those people, that day may have never come.

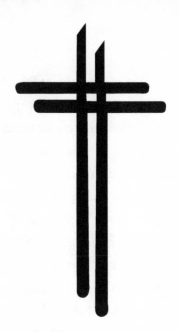

Chapter 5

COMING BACK TO LIFE

BY DAVE

I f you ask me about my time at KMC or the first part of my stay at Rancho Los Amigos, I can only remember bits and pieces. But it was much worse at the time. When I arrived at Rancho, I struggled so badly with my memory that I couldn't recall the medical staff, even if I had met them.

Someone might come up to me and say, "Hi, Dave. I'm your intake nurse. Do you remember me?" And I said, "I'm sorry, I do not." Or someone might say, hi, I'm so-and-so, and I performed this or that procedure or did this or that service. "Do you remember me?" I could never remember.

When I arrived at Rancho, it was like I had lost six to eight years of memories. I thought my fourteen-year-old daughter was seven or eight. My son, five at the time, had not yet been born, at least in my mind. We still lived at our old address. Pets who had long since been gone were still alive.

It was a rough gig, forgetting six-plus years of my life! But it has slowly come back, at least some of it.

The first thing I remember at Rancho was reaching down my neck, feeling the tracheotomy, and taking off the band around my neck. Then I was scolded by the nurse. "You can't do that! Put that back!" Then she grabbed me, put my hands down, and readjusted the apparatus on my neck even tighter than before so I couldn't mess with it. Lesson learned!

The tracheotomy wasn't my only physical concern, not by a long shot. I was still a broken mess. My right ankle was crushed, probably because of the accelerator pedal. All the ribs on my left side were broken. My left lung was deflated. I had Diffuse Axonal Injury (DAI), a closed-skull brain injury. I had a shunt put in my skull to relieve the pressure without a high risk of meningitis. My left shoulder was broken. My back and neck were broken. I ended up with neuropathy as a result.

In addition, the language center of my brain was damaged, causing aphasia. I could clearly see what I wanted to say but couldn't say it. It was immensely frustrating and continues to be that way even today. However, it's slowly getting better. (You may have also read that the actor Bruce Willis also has aphasia.)

Orpha played games to help me. I wouldn't know what a certain store was, so she would say, "You know, the one with the red sign that looks like something you shoot at!"

"Oh yeah, Target!"

She also bought word-find books and once even brought me a book called *Keep Your Brain Alive: 83 Neurobic Exercises to Help*

Prevent Memory Loss and Increase Mental Fitness by Lawrence C. Katz, Ph.D. and Manning Rubin. I believe these and other things stopped my memory loss and improved my ability to process information faster. Those and other tools helped me rewire my brain. I still can't always pick the words I want to say, but it's gotten better.

Learning to swallow was a tough one. The little flap in the back of my throat wouldn't close the airway to my lungs when I swallowed. They were worried I would choke on anything I tried to swallow. One day I had a swallow test at Rancho. Orpha, who is so sweet and supportive, kept calling people and posting on Facebook, asking others to pray that I would pass the swallow test.

However, God told me otherwise. I remember telling Orpha that I prayed as well, and God told me I would not pass the swallow test. I knew people had to see me broken before they would see me healed! I was certain I would not pass this round of swallow tests or any future round. In fact, I never did pass a swallow test!

One of the ladies at KMC, the physician's assistant who Orpha befriended during my stay there, told Orpha that so long as I demonstrated my ability not to lose weight, she would remove the feeding tube from my belly. And I did, so she removed it.

I can swallow, but it does require concentration. I can't chug anything. Sometimes I joke with people that it's a good thing my beerbong days are over!

As much as I have appreciated the doctors and nurses at KMC and Rancho who helped me so much, this whole experience has taught me that Western medicine doesn't have all the answers. And sometimes, medical professionals get things wrong and make mistakes because they are human.

When I was at Rancho, I couldn't sleep at night. I would lie there awake, sometimes until 4:00 or 5:00 a.m. I was unable to roll on my side because of my crushed ankle, but more importantly, I couldn't sleep. It turned out that one of the pills the doctor prescribed was Ritalin, with the final daily dose at 6:00 p.m. No wonder I couldn't sleep! We moved the last dose up to mid-afternoon, and I soon began sleeping peacefully. I no longer fell asleep during visits in the afternoon.

* * *

Exactly forty days after I arrived at Rancho, I could leave. I still had a long way to go and lots of healing to do. My tracheotomy was still sticking out of my neck, and I knew that would be a challenge. Evidently, they had someone die because the person had prematurely taken out their trach and let them eat before they passed the swallow test. That left the staff a little gun-shy.

I remember it was September 15th, the day before our 26th wedding anniversary. Orpha drove us north toward Shell Beach, where we walked along the shore. More precisely, she walked the Strand while pushing me in my wheelchair.

Our first stop post-Rancho was an ear, nose, and throat doctor who removed the trach. He said I might taste a little "glue" while it heals. Boy, that was an understatement! I went to bed that night, tasting what I'd describe as model glue the whole night long.

That was the first of many places I would visit on my road to recovery. Since being at KMC and Rancho Los Amigos, I've been to The Carrick Brain Center in Dallas, Texas; The Centre for Neuro Skills in Bakersfield, California; The Amen Clinic in Edmonds, Washington; Miller Chiropractic in Santa Clarita, California; Stork Spinal Care in Meridian, Idaho; and the Hyperbaric Oxygen Clinic of Idaho, among other places.

When we were at the Centre for Neuro Skills in Bakersfield, they talked to us about my mental state. One of the psychologists told

Orpha, "Dave's intellect was very high, which is why his brain is working properly."

Every once in a while, I would get irritated in rehab, and they would have Orpha come to pick me up. I got so frustrated I would even do things like toss the Monopoly board, which was out of character for me.

One day, she picked me up, and the math teacher came out. He told Orpha, "I just can't work with him anymore."

"What did he do now?"

"He's smarter than me," he said. "His math skills are better than mine. So, I can't really work with him because he has surpassed anything I can teach him." I was happy to hear that I had not completely lost my mind.

One of the most helpful doctors I have visited is Dr. Stork, who is associated with the National Upper Cervical Chiropractic Association (NUCCA). He works on the neck vertebrae only. It's one of my latest and best hopes to reduce or eliminate all the pain medications I'm on. The doctor says I am doing well and straightening out nicely. Orpha says I'm walking taller and straighter. I must admit, I do feel better. There's also the Neuropathy program I'm on at Active Family Chiropractic. It's having some positive impact, for sure. The latest and greatest is The Hyperbaric Oxygen Clinic of Idaho and Dr. Jen—Jennifer Laude, PhD. The burning in my lower legs and feet is on the decline. I may really start to reduce all the pharmaceuticals shortly!

All my appendages are still attached and working for the most part. My left arm and hand mostly work. My left hand and wrist are numb and partially paralyzed. The constant ringing in my ears from tinnitus is a struggle at times. My spleen is gone. I had a feeding tube until mid-November, four months after the accident. I never did pass a swallow test!

I dropped from 225 pounds to 160 pounds. The only way I stayed at least at 160 was that my brother-in-law kept stealing me protein shakes for my feeding tube. The folks at Rancho were very cautious about removing my feeding tube before I was ready. But when the time came, I went back to KMC to have it removed once I proved my weight was stable. I had already been eating "solid" food like Taco Bell and Sonic. And it tasted great! The funny thing was that I despised Taco Bell before this!

The day came for them to take it out. To celebrate, we went to our favorite fish and chips spot before the procedure. It was wonderful, and I kept eating until I couldn't pack in anymore. We then went to KMC to have it removed. Since it's a tube that feeds directly into the stomach, they had to pull both the tube and the balloon out.

The physician's assistant who was going to do the procedure had a young intern with her. She didn't follow the instructions when the PA told her to put a towel over the spot before pulling it out. I did my part and took an extra hydrocodone beforehand, so I was ready. However, the intern wasn't. She pulled it out, and there was a gush of some of the fish and chips, tartar sauce, and malt vinegar. She had black hair, too, which made it even worse for her!

The poor intern stood there, completely shocked, her hair dripping with food. The PA asked the intern, "You want to clean up, and maybe next time, do as you're instructed?" There was never a dull moment in the hospital.

When you come home from a long stay in the hospital, some of the things that seem minor actually turn out to be quite a big deal. For me, it was driving. I didn't know how much I would miss the independence of getting into a car and just going.

It was honestly pretty tough. You might even call it a test of my willingness to learn, adapt, and adjust to a new normal.

God's people have always been tested. The irony of being at KMC for forty days, then being at Rancho Los Amigos for forty days, isn't lost on me. In the Bible, the number forty represents a time of trial, testing, or hardship.

In the creation story, God caused it to rain forty days and forty nights. When Moses killed an Egyptian, he fled to Midian and spent forty years in the desert. Moses spent forty days and forty nights on Mount Sinai. Jesus was tempted for forty days in the desert, and there were forty days between his resurrection and ascension to heaven.

These were times when God called His people to something more difficult yet greater. Looking back on my journey, I have sensed God calling me to use this experience of testing and hardship to glorify His name and draw people closer to Him.

As I continue to recover and heal, I pray that God would soften my heart so I can say the same thing the prophet Isaiah said after he saw a vision of God on his throne. "Here am I. Send me!"

Chapter 6

A HOPE AND A
FUTURE

BY ORPHA

After Dave left KMC and went to Rancho, he wasn't speaking much. Sometimes he would speak a complete sentence, but it was clear there was significant brain damage. We weren't sure if he would ever go back to work. As time passed, a psychologist from Paramount Farms came and spoke to him. You could tell he was checking up on Dave to see where he was in his recovery.

None of us knew what to think regarding him going back to work. Our biggest concern was that he would return to normal days, able to walk again, talk again, and eat without a feeding tube. So, going back to work was never going to be in the cards. I think the Paramount was just showing support in his recovery.

But people were still calling Dave. He had been the VP of Operations for the company, but he wore so many hats it would take more than one man to do his job. It was those who were calling. "Dave, I have a question for you." "Dave, how do I approach this problem?"

One of the reasons we moved away was that they were still relying on him. It was frustrating, and he felt like he had one foot in the door but couldn't truly be there. It was depressing because he loved his job so much. He saw the people there as more than just co-workers. They were his family.

When the accident happened, over a hundred people beat me to the hospital. There were people from his work, church people, kids from the youth group, people from AA, and others. Dave was loved so much by so many. The idea of being stuck in a back office at work bothered him a lot, so we moved to Idaho to rebuild his life and give him a new persona because he wasn't the VP of a big company anymore.

It turned out that it wasn't just Dave who needed a change of scenery. It was all of us.

* * *

The move to Idaho did not come out of the blue. We had already decided to buy a vacation home to spend time in the summer. We had been vacationing there for quite a few years and loved the area.

Dave's car accident was on a Wednesday, and we were planning a trip for that Friday. We had a real estate agent up there, Toni Palmiotto from Garden Valley Properties, who was going to show us a bunch of homes. We planned to buy one and use it for an Airbnb, except for the times we wanted to use it. Of course, that didn't happen, but we just vacationed there and loved it so much.

After Dave's accident, it was a pretty dark time for us. We saw doctors three and four times a week. There was always an appointment we were going to, and it was dragging us all down. So as soon as he got to the point where we didn't have to do that anymore, we wanted to get out of there. It was no longer a good place to be.

The move was our daughter's idea. She was finishing up her junior year of high school when she came to me and said, "We've got to go. Dad's not okay, and I think he would do better in Idaho."

I said, "Well, we have planned to stay one more year for you to finish school."

"No," she said, "We need to leave." So, we took her out of school and moved to Idaho during her junior year. She spent the last part of her junior year and all her senior year here, and she was right. We needed to go. It was just too hard to stay.

I've had a few people ask, "How were your kids during all this?" It was a four-year recovery, and I have no idea how to answer that. I wish I could say I was a great mom the whole time. But truthfully, we were just surviving. I look back and wonder, who raised these kids?

I wasn't a horrible parent by any means, but I wasn't as present as I should have been because I was so concerned about Dave's recovery. Kids aren't blind. They have more insight than we realize. She could see we needed to make a change.

I think she also saw me struggling a bit as well. The whole dynamic of our family and our identity changed overnight. It was almost like someone flipped a switch. I believe she thought that if we left, we could flip it back on again and be better. She was right. It was a good move, a kind of a reinvention of our whole family.

Now that we are established in Idaho, it's interesting that nobody here knows Dave has a brain injury unless he tells them, "Hey, I got in a car accident and am struggling with my words today," or "My leg hurts because of a car accident." Everyone in Bakersfield knew it. The accident was in the newspaper and on TV, and we couldn't go anywhere without someone knowing. Once, we walked into church, and they gave him a standing ovation. "There's Dave Blanchat. He's the one who made it through that horrible car accident."

Sometimes you just need to leave and start forming a new identity. Fortunately, we serve a God who specializes in giving people new identities and fresh starts.

* * *

One of our favorite verses of Scripture is Jeremiah 29:11. "'For I know the plans I have for you,' declares the Lord, 'plans to prosper you and not to harm you, plans to give you hope and a future.'"

Those words were written to God's people well over two thousand years ago. But they're still relevant today, no matter the situation. God doesn't want to harm us. He wants to give us a hope and a future.

I believe our mission is to help spread that message through Dave's story. We want to help people who are struggling, no matter the situation. It might be alcoholism, the loss of a child, the collapse of a marriage, a pandemic, a catastrophic war, or a million other things.

You need to know you can recover from tragedies. You need to understand that you can go through a horrific experience and come out better, stronger, and more resilient on the other side. If you put God first, He will show you how to make it through.

God Shots are not just for Dave or me. They're for everyone, including you. Dave describes himself as "a work in progress," but the truth is, we are *all* works in progress if we continually open ourselves up to what He can teach us through problem-solving, difficult situations, health struggles, relationship challenges, and more. God's not finished with any of us until the day He calls us home to glory.

If you're hungry for the peace, the miracles, and the strength only God can give, we can't wait for you to join us in Part 2 of this book, where you'll learn practical strategies for experiencing God Shots in every area of your life.

DAVE AND HIS KIDS ON A FERRY RIDE
ACROSS THE PUGET SOUND IN WASHINGTON STATE.

DAVE AND PAIGE ON A HIKE TO THE PAINTED CAVE
IN CALIFORNIA'S SANTA BARBARA COUNTY.

(FROM L TO R) NATHAN, CONAN, DAVE & DAVE SZEFLIN ON THEIR RITTER PASS HIKE
OVER THE MINARETS IN CALIFORNIA'S SIERRA MOUNTAINS.

DAVE AFTER HIS 'LONG DISTANCE SHOOT' FINAL.

DAVE'S DODGE RAM 2500 MEGA CAB TRUCK AFTER THE ACCIDENT.

THE SEMI WITH A TANKER TRAILER OF OIL
THAT DEMOLISHED DAVE'S TRUCK.

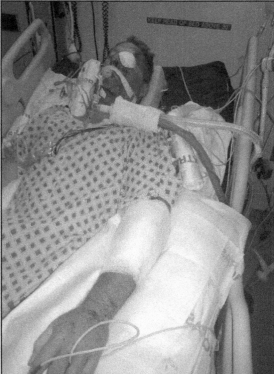

DAVE IN THE ICU
AT KERN MEDICAL CENTER (KMC).

DAVE IN THE ICU OF KMC.
HIS EYE WAS DAMAGED
& IT LOOKED AS THOUGH
A BEAR HAD MAULED
THE LEFT SIDE OF HIS FACE.

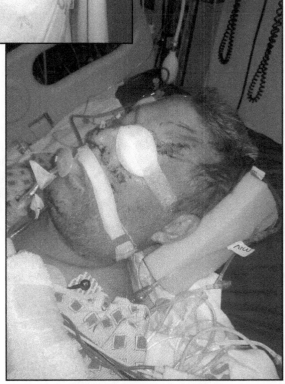

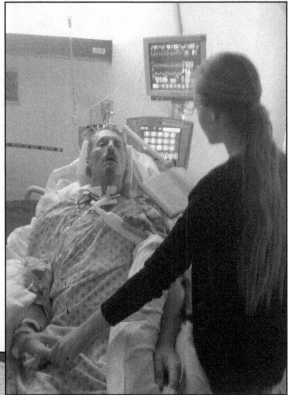

PAIGE READING STREAMS IN THE DESERT TO HER DAD IN THE ICU.

ONE OF THE WINDOWED WALLS IN DAVE'S ROOM OF THE ICU. HIS ENTIRE ROOM WAS ADORNED THIS WAY!

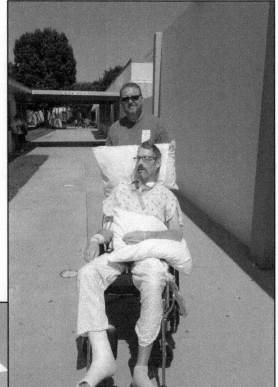

ORVAL, DAVE'S BROTHER-IN-LAW, TAKING HIM FOR A WALK OUTSIDE RANCHO LAS AMIGOS IN DOWNEY, CA. AT THE TIME, DAVE'S LEFT HAND AND ARM WERE USELESS AND HIS HEAD COMPLETELY UNSTABLE.

DAVE WITH HIS PHYSICAL THERAPIST (L) AND JOHN FERGUSON (R), A FANTASTIC COLLEGE FRIEND, AT RANCHO LOS AMIGOS.

DAVE AND ORPHA BEFORE A BRAD PAISLEY CONCERT IN BOISE, IDAHO.

PAIGE, DAVE, & DAVID AT BREAKFAST IN HORSESHOE BEND, IDAHO.

DAVE & DAVID HUNTING
IN GARDEN VALLEY, IDAHO.

LANCE (L) & DAVE (R)
IN BAKERSFIELD, CALIFORNIA.

DAVE & DAVID HUNTING
IN GARDEN VALLEY, IDAHO.

LANCE (L) & DAVE (R)
IN BAKERSFIELD, CALIFORNIA.

Part 2

KEYS TO A SUCCESSFUL LIFE

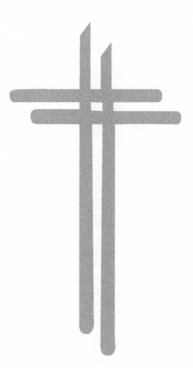

Chapter 7

ATTITUDE: SEEING LIFE WITH THE CORRECT PERSPECTIVE

BY DAVE

I f you have stuck with us this far in the book, you have read my story in detail. You know about my accident, the thirty-day coma, and the long recovery, which will never be fully finished. I will always be recovering in one way or another from the horrific accident that shattered my body—and my life—that summer day back in 2014.

But just like the ancient mythological image of a phoenix rising from the ashes, I have determined to rise from the brokenness of this accident and soar to new heights. But I don't want to fly alone. I want you to fly with me.

This book isn't really about me. It's about you. We are using my story as a springboard to talk about critical issues for men and women. No matter your age, life experience, marital and family status, or background, you need to start recognizing the God Shots in your life. You need a fresh infusion of God's grace, power, and insight so you can soar to new heights as well.

But where do you begin? How do you build a new life and experience those God Shots for yourself? I believe it all starts with the right attitude. *Attitude* is one of those words that is casually tossed around but is rarely defined. Let's take a moment to make sure we are on the same page.

Have you ever been in the market for a new pair of glasses because you can't see clearly? Vision is a pretty critical element of our lives. If you can't see, it's hard to do anything else. When your vision is limited or gone altogether, it's hard to drive, walk, or avoid potential disasters lurking around the corner.

When you visit the eye doctor, go through an eye exam, and finally receive your new glasses, it's like the whole world has opened up again! Everything is more crisp. You can see details again. You can avoid running into things. You have reduced your headaches.

I witnessed it firsthand while on a construction and medical team mission trip to Honduras. One of the tasks we were assigned there was to finish work on a vocational school and provide much-needed medical and ophthalmologist help. During lunch, I had the opportunity to witness an older gentleman being escorted, as if he couldn't see where he was going, into a room being used for eye exams. From my vantage point several feet away, I could see them all clearly but couldn't hear them, which was fine since they were speaking Spanish anyway, and I just knew enough to be dangerous.

After a bit, the man shuffled out, escorted by the ophthalmologist's son. He was led to his family, where a few things happened that left a mark on me to this day. The Hispanic gentleman pulled a white Styrofoam envelope out of his breast pocket; it held a pair of glasses. Several pairs were donated back in the states, collected up, and sent ahead of time to Honduras, where they'd be "fitted" to the right prescription.

He put them on, looked around in bewilderment, and raised his hands high toward heaven. His family marveled with their hands over their mouths. He then took off the glasses, put them back in their Styrofoam shield, placed them in his pocket, and the whole family shuffled out of the building. We were serving as Christ's hands and feet, giving sight to the near-blind!

A good attitude is like having new glasses for your entire life. When you have the right attitude—or rather, the right set of attitudes—you get a whole new perspective on life. More importantly, you get *God's* perspective on life.

Your attitude is critical because you don't get to choose what happens to you in life. You can change your circumstances and try to put yourself in the right situation where good things are happening, but random events happen . . . like auto accidents.

Even if you have planned and prepared to the best of your ability, life happens. People get hurt. Your best-laid plans come crashing down. And in those moments, your attitude will either make or break you.

In those moments, God can miraculously intervene. But wouldn't it be great to live a kind of life where you see God more clearly every day? How could you adjust your attitude and perspective so you can open your life to even more God Shots?

The Apostle Paul gives us a helpful point of view and great practical advice in Philippians 4:4-9.

Rejoice in the Lord always. I will say it again: Rejoice! Let your gentleness be evident to all. The Lord is near. Do not be anxious about anything, but in every situation, by prayer and petition, with thanksgiving, present your requests to God. And the peace of God, which transcends all understanding, will guard your hearts and your minds in Christ Jesus.

Finally, brothers and sisters, whatever is true, whatever is noble, whatever is right, whatever is pure, whatever is lovely, whatever is admirable—if anything is excellent or praiseworthy—think about such things. Whatever you have learned or received or heard from me, or seen in me—put it into practice. And the God of peace will be with you.

In the rest of this chapter, we will look at four attitudes to help you see life with the correct perspective and inject more God Shots into your everyday life.

I. AN ATTITUDE OF JOY

Paul tells us to "rejoice in the Lord always." But is that possible in an age when we are constantly seeking things to fulfill our every whim?

Most people equate joy with happiness, but they are not the same thing. Happiness depends on circumstances. When things are going well, when you get a raise, when everyone is healthy, and when you don't have any major problems, it's easy to be happy.

The world would have you believe that happiness is your goal, but it's not true. The true goal is joy, which is greater than happiness. Joy comes from a good relationship with Jesus and doesn't depend on circumstances. You can be joyful at all times.

If you look at the verses that come a little later in Philippians 4, you will learn how to be content in every situation, regardless of what is happening around you. ". . . for I have learned to be content whatever the circumstances. I know what it is to be in need, and I know what it is to have plenty. I have learned the secret of being content in any and every situation, whether well fed or hungry, whether living in plenty or in want. I can do all this through him who gives me strength." (Philippians 4:11b-13).

Can you say that about yourself? Can you be content no matter what is going on in your life, no matter the external circumstances?

One of the biggest barriers to joy is a lack of forgiveness. If you hold a grudge against someone, it will rob you of your joy. You cannot be bitter, judgmental, or angry and be joyful at the same time. It's simply not possible.

If you have trouble forgiving someone, think of it this way; wouldn't it be terrible if God held all your wrongdoing over your head and refused to forgive you? What if there were "strings attached" to His love and forgiveness? That would be a terrible way to live, yet we do the same thing all the time to others when we refuse to forgive them.

I confess that it was hard for me to forgive the man who hit me with his truck and nearly killed me. Talk about someone inflicting harm on you and your family! Yet over time, with God's help, I forgave him. What a weight lifted off my chest!

It's not only essential to forgive others. We must also forgive ourselves. Hanging onto guilt and shame will steal your joy just as much as a refusal to forgive others. Read Luke chapter 15 and get re-acquainted with the story of the prodigal son. In the story, the father embraced his son, who had wandered far away. Always remember, no matter how far away from God you have gone, He will always run to meet you when you want to come home.

When you can let go of the burdens weighing you down and embrace true joy, it's an attitude that makes a huge difference in your life.

2. AN ATTITUDE OF GENTLENESS

Philippians 4:5 says, "Let your gentleness be evident to all. The Lord is near." Gentleness is often seen as a weakness, which is why so many guys try to be "manly men" to show how tough they are. But gentleness doesn't mean being weak or being "less than." Rather, a real man or woman knows when to be gentle and treat people with the sensitivity and respect they deserve. It means being empathetic and learning to act in a way that considers other people's points of view.

I faced this situation several years ago when I ran Operations at Wonderful. One of the metrics we used to determine our success was TIR, or "Total Incident Rate." It was the rate of incidents that injured or even killed people. When running a huge operation like Wonderful that uses huge machines, warehouses, and heavy equipment, you will always have accidents because that is human nature. But despite our best efforts to create a safe environment, our TIR was going in the wrong direction.

For example, one time, a worker crushed someone with a fork-lift. During harvest time, the trash from the pistachio huller would go into bins, which would be loaded onto forklifts later in the process. That particular employee was trying to put the bin on the floor, but it wouldn't go down. They kept trying, not knowing there was someone underneath the bin. Obviously, that was a problem.

Even though we had many safety protocols, such as yellow lines on the floor indicating safety areas and many other measures and regulations, people were still getting hurt. Even though safety was not my job directly, I was still running the whole operation, so it was still my responsibility. In addition, I was the one who might have to inform family members that their child, spouse, or parent had gotten injured or worse.

Neither employees nor management was handling the situation appropriately. Whenever these incidents happened, they would respond in a punitive way—in other words, punishing people on the back end rather than working toward better prevention on the front end. They also thought in terms of some kind of physical or mechanical fix for the situation rather than looking at the human element.

The whole situation was tearing me up because I really cared about our operation and our employees, not to mention the emotional stress that happens when someone gets injured on your watch or you have to attend a funeral for one of them. It's gut-wrenching! Nearly every day, when I drove to work in the morning and when I came home in the evening, I prayed, "Lord, please protect the employees. Keep them safe from injury and illness." That situation was very close to my heart.

One morning, I was taking a shower, crying like a baby, and asking God for direction because I felt like I was failing my people. God said to me, "Make them feel your pain. Let your people know how this affects you and makes you feel."

As I thought more about God's instruction to me, I came up with an idea.

I gathered people in groups of twenty or thirty and had them stand across from each other in pairs. Each person had to tell their partner the name of a close family member (or, in some cases, a family member who worked there). Then they had to shake their hand and say, "I'm sorry to inform you that your son or daughter [insert the employee's kid's name] has been killed in an accident at our operation."

It was an effective way to help people empathize with the injuries and death that could happen because of carelessness or not following safety protocols. People were actually crying, having to pretend they were telling someone their son, daughter, or family member had been killed.

In dealing with the problem of safety, I took the "gentle" approach instead of the harsh one. That simple exercise changed a lot of attitudes, including mine and the senior folks of the company. You can get things done with harsh behavior, but gentleness is much more effective because you can speak to people's hearts. After that, things like safety bonuses were implemented to continue the domino effect.

3. AN ATTITUDE OF GRATITUDE

In Philippians 4:6, there is a little word tucked away you might have missed—thanksgiving. It's more than a holiday we celebrate once a year. Thanksgiving—or gratitude—is a way of life.

My AA sponsor, John, gave me a heaping dose of reality one day when we were at camp for the annual Broken Neck Trout Campout for men. The event was started by a few guys trying to keep another guy sober. Except for 2020, when so many other events were cancelled, it has been going for several decades straight.

We had been flyfishing at a lake earlier that day, and I was complaining about how sore, tired, and generally irritated I was. I couldn't even get in and out of the float tube by myself. That was the wrong thing to say to John . . . or perhaps it was the right thing to say!

He said, "At least you get to do this. I have no idea how you feel, and I pray I never do, but I know a pity party when I hear one. You weren't the only one affected by your accident. Think about that, and get outside yourself. What about Orpha, your kids, and many others who were affected?"

Phew, John was right! Soon afterward, I set out to make a gratitude list. Here are some of the items I listed:

1. My life. Thank you, Lord!
2. All my appendages, most of them in working order
3. My wife, Orpha

4. My son, David
5. My daughter, Paige
6. My friends
7. Alcoholics Anonymous
8. Meetings
9. Fishing kayaks and float tubes
10. I can fish, hunt, & walk about. Not hike like I used to, but I can hike some!
11. My brain still works, for the most part. At the time, I hadn't yet come to grips with the severity of my brain injury
12. My sobriety . . . I don't have to drink
13. My humor (ask Paige, I'm a funny fella!).
14. Steak
15. Love
16. Laughter
17. Our then-planned new life in Idaho and getting out of California!
18. Sunrises
19. Sunsets
20. Kid's laughter
21. Christmas
22. Easter
23. The list goes on!

If you have never made a gratitude list, give it a try. I promise this one little act of list-making will change your entire perspective on life and put you in the right frame of mind.

4. AN ATTITUDE OF AFFIRMATION

We don't use the word "affirmation" very much in everyday conversations. That is a shame because it's a vital concept that can revolutionize your relationships and your perspective.

Paul encourages us to think about things that are true, noble, right, pure, lovely, and admirable (Philippians 4:8). We are to *affirm* these things, dwell upon them, and put them in the forefront of our minds.

But that doesn't happen by accident. We have to actively look for the good, the true, and the honorable in the world around us and in other people.

We had an employee, Ernie, who wanted to be our Safety Manager. Ernie came to me one day and said, "I'd like to put my name in the hat for the job."

"Thank you," I said. "Just be aware that the job requires you to have a four-year degree." Ernie didn't have a degree, so he couldn't apply for the job right then. But later on, I heard that he had enrolled in a university to get a four-year degree in business. He had been running the mobile maintenance shop for me.

I called him into my office one day and said, "I heard you're going back to school to get your degree." He said it was true and started telling me about it. I said, "The job is yours if you want it."

That wouldn't have happened if I had only been looking for people who were qualified right then. I chose to look deeper into Ernie's attitude and his incredible work ethic. Because of that, he could step into a role with more responsibility.

The opposite can be true as well. Sometimes I had guys come to me for a job, and they had a fantastic resume with all kinds of excellent work experience. However, their attitude was lacking, and I wouldn't hire them. Sometimes you don't have to look too far to find the truth about someone.

THE POWER OF YOUR EXAMPLE

If you are reading this, you are a leader. Whether you run a company or stay home with your kids, you lead others. It's one thing to raise the level of your own attitude, but it's quite another to try and help those you lead to develop a better attitude. As we move toward the home stretch in this chapter, I would like to offer some thoughts for every leader.

When you have an employee or team member who has a problematic attitude, how do you handle them?

I have always told team members to work out their personal issues through a counselor or friend. They should never take their anger or frustration out on other people, especially at work. I would offer to help them put together a plan, direct them to someone who could help, or challenge them to leave those issues at the door when they walk in.

Sometimes, there is a fine line between caring for people and enabling their destructive behavior or attitude. A good leader can tell the difference and knows how to address a delicate situation.

A good team member needs to be "all in." They cannot go back out there and stay in the same "Debbie Downer" mode, or it will create a toxic environment. You can help people to a certain extent, but at some point, they need to take ownership and responsibility for themselves.

However, it begins with you as the leader, setting a good example. Have you done a gut check and examined your own attitude? Have you brought your best self to work—and for that matter, to your home? It's hard for people at work to be their best if their leaders are not demonstrating the right attitude.

Notice what Philippians 4:9 says. "Whatever you have learned or received or heard from me, or seen in me—put it into practice. And the God of peace will be with you." Paul pointed to himself as an example that others should follow. That is what all good leaders do.

When I was a younger leader in my thirties, I saw a great illustration of leadership that has stuck with me ever since. Lay a shoelace or piece of string on the table and try to push it from the back end. What happens to the string? It binds up and goes in different directions. You can push the string where you want it to go, but only by brute force.

Now pull the string from the front. What happens? It lines up perfectly and goes wherever you direct it with minimal friction. That is the definition of good leadership.

A lot of people who believe they are leaders are not. They are managers. They manage (push) people to get them to that point. But leaders pull people by coaching, training, and, most of all, by setting a great example with the right attitude.

When I came out of my coma, the world was a blur. I had lost several years from my memory. It took me a long time to even learn how to loop my belt into my pants properly. There was a long process of re-learning things I once knew.

You may have a long way to go, too. Maybe you have not been in a terrible car accident, but you have challenges, nonetheless. With the right attitude and God's help, you will be amazed at what you can accomplish.

GOD SHOTS FOR SUCCESS

1. On a scale of 1-10, how joyful do you feel in your life right now? Are you able to experience joy even in the challenges of life? Be as honest as you can.
2. Think of someone in your life who is causing you frustration. What can you do to be gentler and more patient with him or her?
3. Take a moment right now to make a list of five things you are thankful for.
4. What are three qualities in your family, friends, or co-workers you can affirm? Have you told them about the positive qualities you see in them?

Chapter 8

MARRIAGE: STAYING COMMITTED TO YOUR SPOUSE

BY DAVE

Imagine your favorite author reformatting one of their books, so the entire story is crammed onto two pages. How many problems would it create for you as a reader? The font would be too tiny to read, and eventually, the words would start to overlap. Every story needs fresh pages to keep going.

In the same way, marriages stop growing when they are not able to turn pages and continue. Couples turn pages and add to their unique marriage story with acts of forgiveness, changing attitudes, aligning priorities, and other acts of mutual growth. Characters in every story have problems to overcome. That is what makes the story come alive.

Whenever we see characters handle problems correctly, we learn how to handle our own problems more effectively.

Christian couples listening to the Lord have a "bonus author" who can help them write a story that would be impossible without His touch. God Shots in our marriage make our story special. We've had our ups and downs, and God has helped us build a marriage that lasts. Alcoholism, workaholism, losing an infant, and Dave's accident are all pages we've turned together. We choose to keep writing our love story with Jesus, and it keeps getting better and better.

What would happen to you if God showed up in your marriage? How do you respond when the Lord does not give the God Shot you want but offers a different path for your marriage to grow? Do you have trouble "turning the page" on difficult parts of your marriage? Have you and your spouse stopped writing your story because it is too hard and painful?

Our marriage story is one we've shared with a number of people. We've been through a lot together and trust that these God Shots we can share with you will help you and your spouse write your love story.

GROWING UP TOGETHER

Orpha and I were high school sweethearts, and we got married at the ripe old age of twenty-one. I am one week older than Orpha, and we've lived more of our lives together than separately. We were best friends in high school as we attended dances, celebrated football games, and graduated together in our class of thirty-two students!

Neither of us comes from a great family situation. My parents divorced when I was eleven, and I grew up with my dad in Oregon. My sister lived with Mom in Washington. Mom did her best. She's a strong lady who worked multiple jobs to get us off welfare. That was always meant to be a hand-up, not a hand-out.

Dad was absent for much of my childhood, but he later became a good father and a good grandparent to our kids. He loved to have fun with our son David. Mom's still with us but Dad has since passed away. Mom and Dad always did the best they knew, and I am thankful for them both.

Orpha grew up with a terrible family life and struggled with undiagnosed ADD. She was just trying to survive and ended up moving out when she was sixteen. With no parental supervision, she was a bit of a lost child.

Although we both had our own experiences growing up in our households, Orpha and I had to create our own model for our marriage and family life. I did not want my kids to have the same childhood and teenage years I experienced. The place it had to start was in our marriage. By God's grace, Orpha and I found each other.

Marriage is forever, not just until one or both spouses feel like calling it quits. We had to learn to grow our marriage, even through the struggles of infidelity, alcohol addiction, the death of Sarah Anne, and other crises that should have ended our relationship. But they did not, thanks to Orpha, not me!

I grew up in a divorced family, but we're breaking the cycle. Divorce in our generation ends here, with us, in the everyday "here and now" of our lives. Our vision of family is not something that accidentally happened to us. Our marriage today comes from how we chose to grow through each and every obstacle, flaw, sin, and failure. 'Til death do us part, in sickness and in health, is a commitment we live every day—not just words we spoke on our wedding day.

FINDING JESUS TOGETHER

Jesus saved us as a married couple in our thirties when Orpha and I decided to attend church. We weren't sure which church to try, so we picked the one our nice next-door neighbors attended.

The first service we attended was the play *Heaven's Gates and Hell's Flames*. The play chronicles the experiences of people going to heaven or hell. It was an intense service, not for the faint of heart!

There's a scene in the play featuring an airplane full of people. As we were watching, suddenly, the lights flickered, and they all went out. When the lights came back on, only a few people were left in the airplane. Some folks were called to heaven, and the others were left on earth to deal with what was coming next.

The play made me realize I needed to do something for my soul right then and there. The play ended, and my wife went down to the altar area in the front with me close behind. I couldn't wait to give my life to Christ!

TURNING PAGES TO WRITE THE STORY OF YOUR MARRIAGE

Orpha and I had to learn marriage lessons by being married. There are no shortcuts to making loving decisions day in and day out. Sometimes, we don't get it right. Our marriage did not start and grow on a straight path; yours won't either.

The Apostle Paul gives a good picture of your marriage in Ephesians 5:25-33. The focus is not on where we start but on what our marriage can become so that it can reflect God's heart for the church and the world.

Husbands, love your wives, just as Christ loved the church and gave himself up for her to make her holy, cleansing her by the washing with water through the word, and to present her to himself as a radiant church, without stain or wrinkle or any other blemish, but holy and blameless. In this same way, husbands ought to love their wives as their own bodies. He who loves his wife loves himself. After all, no one ever hated their own body, but they feed and care for their body, just as Christ does the church—for we are members of his body. "For this reason a man will leave his father and mother and be united to his wife, and the two will become one flesh." This is a profound mystery—but I am talking about Christ and the church. However, each one of you also must love his wife as he loves himself, and the wife must respect her husband.

Let's look at several principles to help us honor marriage and uphold the ideals Paul shares with us in these verses.

I. BE WILLING TO CHANGE YOURSELF

According to Paul, Jesus is actively "cleansing" the church so that she will be "without stain or wrinkle or any other blemish, but holy and blameless." *Cleansing* is a way of saying "set apart" or "purified." Those goals require change and growth to become something new—the bride of Jesus.

Change is part of marriage. You will change. Your spouse will change and grow as a person. There is no question about the reality of change. It's just a question of how we will manage and grow with change in our marriage.

Some changes in our marriage have been great. Orpha and I became followers of Jesus, we have great kids, and we made a new family life in Idaho. Don't get me wrong, these were not easy changes, but they were good—even great—changes for us.

Other changes come from hard places. With a TBI (Traumatic Brain Injury), my warning signs for "trouble" became different. I now have anxiety and anger issues that can flash in an instant. As a result, my anger and anxiety precautions had to become different. I ended up deleting all my social media accounts. At one point, I thought I could manage the social media environment, but in the end, I could not. My online life was too toxic, and it affected my home life. So, it was out.

I decided it was better to lose stuff like Facebook and Instagram than lose my family.

2. SEEK YOUR SPOUSE'S HAPPINESS

Jesus is making the church complete, whole, and ready to present to the Father; he holds nothing back from us. Paul tells husbands to love their wives as they "love their own bodies." Our bodies and minds are pretty amazing pieces of creation. Ignoring our hunger only lasts so long before we might even do illegal things to feed ourselves and protect our lives.

Are you starving your spouse? We all know Jesus is providing more than physical food to us. He promises to be with us and help us find joy, purpose, direction, and fulfillment. Notice Paul's focus on how Jesus cares for the church to bring about change and doesn't just provide a list of demands or consequences for the church that refuses to change. Do we love our spouse the same way Jesus loves the church?

A helpful way to think about our spouse's happiness is to think of our relationship like a checking account—a checking account that does not gain interest on its own and even has a negative interest rate! It's a worthwhile account, trust me. No matter how much you start with, if you spend and spend and spend and refuse to make regular deposits, it will reach $0 and become negative. Your checking account requires constant deposits to stay positive!

If you're thinking of a relationship with your significant other, think of it as earning negative interest. So, you need to make constant deposits of different acts of love. I know this is a simple formula, but it's hard to do!

I've found that keeping a bunch of cards on your home desk for birthdays, anniversaries, missed occasions, or whatever happens to anyone in your immediate extended family! Buy 'em and keep 'em handy. You'll be glad you did. I pick some up anytime Orpha and I are in a drug store or Hallmark Store, then add them to my stash.

Even though I know I am more sentimental than Orpha, and sending cards is not necessarily her love language, I know she appreciates the gesture. It is important to remember that even though your spouse may not always get things exactly right, they are trying.

In addition to expressions of love with such gifts, I've also found that sharing hobbies with your spouse will fill your soul and give you peace—in other words, hobbies that will involve both you and your spouse. Orpha and I went diving together. Why? I was the diver. Her, not at all! But we dove because she made the sacrifice. Orpha says her love for me is greater than her fear of the water, and she is terrified of the water! Me; I don't like shopping, and I don't like china place settings, but I love spending time with my wife, so guess what; I now love shopping for china!

The key is to find and do something you can learn to have fun with together or invent new shared hobbies. Some ideas include:

Long walks on peaceful nights
Ice cream
Lunch dates
Game nights, which are very fun, especially when kids are involved!
Surprise notes throughout the house
Random calls to your "other" at home or at their job
Little gifts, cards, and what-notes left throughout the home or their office
Notes with "redeemable" coupons!
Getaway weekends
Movie nights
Surprises and "just because" gifts like gift cards, flowers, and such
A date night where *she* is the prize and knows it!

I know what you are thinking. You've heard all this before. We all have. But are you implementing these suggestions? Give them a try!

3. LET YOUR SPOUSE CARE FOR YOU

"Becoming one flesh" is an act of submitting ourselves to receiving one another. Paul said Jesus is making this mystery of becoming one, of true unity, come true for the church. But what happens to the church if she refuses the gifts of Jesus? The relationship will break.

Many people keep away and, tragically, walk away from Jesus because of hurt and wrong ideas. A lifetime of hurts allows Jesus to keep overcoming our sins and the sins others have committed against us.

No one in a marriage is perfect like Jesus. I've done many things that would justify Orpha saying, "That's it, I'm done!" But she chose to turn the pages of our marriage and keep writing our story. She chose to leave would-be issues at the foot of the cross. She let me grow and change, and she lets me keep on loving her. A major part of forgiveness between spouses is trusting and allowing our spouse to love us after they have hurt or disappointed us.

4. REMEMBER THAT PAIN IS PART OF LIFE, BUT SUFFERING IS A CHOICE

In over thirty years of marriage, we've learned that life is full of pain, but suffering is a choice. The pain of your spouse's failure can be devastating, but it does not need to remain constant suffering. Remember, Jesus is helping you write a marriage that will make you and your spouse "sanctified" and bring honor and glory to the Father.

Let me share two quick words on forgiveness and making a new life with your spouse.

First, some marriages need to dissolve for the safety of the spouse and children. I know this is a controversial issue with some people, but it seems pretty cut and dried when people's safety and security are involved.

Second, when the pain is great, it is wise to speak with a mediator. You need to rely on someone who can help guide you to the promises of God. Your pastor, a counselor, or a trusted friend can help you come together again in Christ. If you are so angry at each other or so hurt you can't talk to each other, then start by talking to your mediator separately.

Trust God to overcome any sin in your life and marriage. Paul says Jesus is in the full-time business of sanctifying us, and that includes your marriage. The ability to turn the page and write more for your marriage comes from a place of faith. If you have faith that you can get your marriage and spouse back, you can solve the problems and save your marriage.

That is why it is so important to seek counsel from someone who can help focus on faith. Seek a mediator who can give you the belief in yourself and each other. If you don't see and have the same goal, you will never reach it together.

Please, please talk to someone before you decide to go down the road of divorce. Once you go down that road, it will cause a whole bunch of other issues you might not expect. It will affect your kids in a huge way. What are the visitations going to be like? You will also need to think about the house and physical assets. What's going to happen to them? This is all stuff that gets complicated if you decide to divorce.

Orpha and I realized there are worse things in life than stopping our marriage story and getting divorced. What keeps us together is being a team. So, figure out what the other person needs, mentally and physically, and then deliver that to each other. Then, receive it from each other.

5. COMMUNICATE A NEW FUTURE

Jesus's actions of love and care for his bride, the church, do not take into account where we start or where He finds us. His care is to take us from where we are and love us into what we need to become.

Mine and Orpha's broken home lives did not determine the success of our marriage. Moral failure, alcohol, the death of our daughter, and a serious accident in our marriage did not determine the success of our marriage.

Our choices have been to turn over pages and keep writing new chapters together. And again, I think it's very important to be a team. You can't short-cut your way into a healthy marriage. You need to talk out your problems and not hide from each other. Making a life together means each spouse does not try to do it on their own.

Talking to each other does not have to be complicated. I can go to Orpha and just say, "Hey, this is what I'm working on, and this is why. What do you think?" She will think about it and might say, "Well, that's pretty good. Good job." Or, she might say, "No, this is what I think you should do."

Writing a story together is not just about getting over hard things. It is also about receiving good things together.

A GOD SHOT FOR OUR NEW HOME

The story of our homes is a God Shot that included Orpha and I talking and working with one another. Our goal for many years has been to retire in Idaho—God's country! We vacationed there in Garden Valley some years back. That first visit led to more visits and vacations. In fact, we were planning a trip to Idaho two days after my accident in 2014.

We finally made that trip but did not find our retirement house. Orpha and I went on a house hunt in 2017 while I was still using a cane. We found a house that would work for our family but not the retirement home of our hopes and dreams. It was just a house in the mountains, but God had something else in mind for us. We prayed before we went to look at homes, knowing "faith brings a basket to market."

One night, Orpha prayed to God about this mountain house we had made an offer on, and then she went to sleep. She woke with God's audible voice telling her that the house was not in our basket. Orpha told me to withdraw our offer when the sellers made a counter-offer. When that happened, I asked our agent to pull our offer. She was surprised and reminded us, "But you've been looking so long!" I told her, "Orpha has this on the highest authority!"

The agent called us back, bubbling with excitement less than two hours later. A log home was just listed, the kind that rarely becomes available! A log home, the type that never resells. A log home that was Orpha's dream home could be ours. Here's the real kicker; we had toured the home earlier and reserved it for an upcoming Blanchat Family Reunion!

Yeah, that house never held the reunion. We bought it!

But we had forgotten some details. Like, it was three floors; the master bedroom is at the top . . ., and the laundry facilities in the basement level. But we had the home God wanted for us, and it moved us to Idaho. But, of course, there is more to the story.

One day in 2019, I turned to Orpha and said, "Hey, let's go ahead and find a place on the river." She looked at me. "Seriously?!"

Orpha had always wanted a house on the river. She'd been hinting at it for years, but I wasn't listening. I wanted a house in the mountains and would be happy with our house, but I wanted her to finally have that house on the river. You might say that was smacking me upside my head, and God was up to something—turning our pain into His purpose.

We drove around and found ourselves at the river house we first wanted to buy when we came to Idaho. While we were sorting ourselves and thinking about placing an offer, a lady bought the house. Disappointed, we looked around and wandered over to the house next door—the "one that got away."

A gentleman came out and asked, "What are you doing? Can I help you?"

"We are trespassing," I said, and then asked, "When are you selling this dump?"

He laughed and said something like, "I'll die in this house!" Basically, he said, "never," so we shook hands and parted ways.

We prayed over that house for years. In fact, Orpha would drive by once a week and pray over it. We prayed as they picked house colors—that they would choose the ones we liked. She would say, "Okay, God, let's go with gray," and then they would move on to selecting the trim colors. Orpha's prayer was for the green.

They would be planting flowers, and she thanked God for the yellows and oranges they put into the front flower bed. Faith brings dreams into reality. She would ask God for that house or something better.

One year later, that couple walked into our realtor's office and said they wanted to sell their home. "Guess what? They want to give first dibs to that 'nice young couple' they had met who was trespassing on the property next door!"

We toured the house, loved it, and made an offer. We felt that all the stuff they were working on that year had been for us. They countered, and we accepted. We were fully convinced that what He had promised, He was (and is) able to perform (Romans 4:21). We continued to see God's hand when we moved again—a story I'll get to later on.

When we write the story with the Lord, he will give us God Shots. Your God Shot may not be a house, but you can be sure that God wants to delight and surprise you.

GOD SHOTS FOR SUCCESS

1. How well do you make space for change and growth in your marriage? Spend a few minutes in prayer reflecting on how you and your spouse have changed since you said, "I do." Are there growth areas you need to address?

2. What makes your spouse happy and content? What things do you do together to fill up their bank account? Are you good at letting your spouse fill up your bank account?

3. How well do you turn the pages of the past as a spouse and together as a couple? Marriage is all about forgiving and getting back to the work of writing your love story.

4. What are you both writing about your marriage right now? Are you on the same page? How is God a coauthor in your marriage story?

Chapter 9

PARENTING: RAISING AMAZING KIDS

BY DAVE

Why would we give up our dream house on the river in beautiful Idaho? You know some of our stories and how much this house means to Orpha and me, so what would make us give it up? And why would I bring that up in a chapter on parenting?

This story starts on a regular Wednesday night in a prayer meeting at church. Once a month, our home church, an hour and a half south, near Boise, sets aside a Wednesday night to offer prayers of healing. On the night of one of those meetings, I was overcome with so many emotions, bouncing from absolute hope in Christ to despair over so much loss from my accident. For others who have long-term mental, physical, or emotional struggles, you know the honest struggle of faith when you are waiting for healing. So, it was for me that night. I was just plain tired of going and asking for help. It started as a really hard night, and I'm going to turn the rest of the story over to Orpha.

* * *

BY ORPHA

I watched Dave praying, and my good friend Jacki leaned over and asked, "Why did Dave not go up for prayer?" I told her that he was tired of going up again and again for prayer. He just wanted to sit and pray in his seat. Jacki went over, placed her hands on Dave, and started praying.

Our son, David, was with us in the healing service. David looked up at me and asked, "Mom, what's going on?" So, I explained to my twelve-year-old son about healing prayer. He was listening to me and watching people at the altar engaged in intense prayer and said, "This is kinda awkward."

David scrunched down in his seat, pulled his ball cap over his eyes, and quietly let crocodile tears run down his cheeks. He asked to go to the restroom, and after a few minutes, he came back into the room and put his head on his dad's shoulder. David was not able to hold it together. He sat there crying on his dad's shoulder. But he was also praying.

The prayer service lasted for a long time that night. I'm sure that Jacki prayed for at least forty minutes with Dave. We sat there; me, Jacki, David, and Dave, after the prayer time, waiting for the service to finish. David still had his eyes cast down to the floor and his ball cap pulled down low. I felt for him and wondered what was going on in his mind.

After the service, Dave drove home in his truck, and I drove home with David in my car. When he got into the car, he was a little bit hysterical, with laughter and crying coming from his mouth at the same time.

"Oh, gosh, David! Are you okay?"

"Something weird happened, mom. I was praying over dad, and you know, I had my eyes closed. And there's a vision of a puzzle."

I thought, *hmm, okay . . .*

"So, these puzzle pieces were dropping down. The puzzle pieces were you, and me, and Paige, and the animals, you know, the animals at our house. There was a missing piece to the puzzle, and it didn't drop for a while. A long minute or so later, it dropped in, and it was Dad."

Then David shared what was eating at him in church. "I realized that I haven't been including God in the puzzle of our life because I'm scared Dad's going to die. I'm scared of the person he's become. And it's so different now, you know, after the accident. I haven't been letting Dad in, and I need to love him as much as I love you and Paige."

David was crying, and I was, too. I was trying to drive, and suddenly, he started laughing. He began a weird, hysterical laugh, and I asked, "Why are you laughing?"

"Well, I think that God has called me to be a pastor."

We spent the next few months encouraging Little David in his calling to be a pastor, but he had it in his mind to be a pastor right then! He was only twelve, and that seemed a little early for us to start letting people know about his passion for becoming a pastor.

During that time of waiting, our pastor agreed to take David to a men's retreat. Dave had a trip scheduled and couldn't go, but Pastor Allen wanted David to attend. He told me (Orpha), "You know, I really think he has an anointing on him. I saw him at the youth retreat, and after he prayed by himself for forty-five minutes, he went around praying with other students."

Well, who doesn't want their kid to spend extra time with the pastor, especially when that kid feels called to the same work? So, David went along with another twelve-year-old and had a great time with the guys.

The weekend drew to a close with prayer time, and David asked Pastor Allen and Pastor Anthony if he could say a few words. David got up and said a word over all the men of the church. He told the men, "You are worried about being a good dad. If you are teaching your children to love their heavenly father, then you're doing a good job." His words moved all the men, and they were bawling.

David said he didn't remember what he said. Pastor Allen told us that is one way you know you are working with anointing and not just a feeling.

* * *

BY DAVE

And that's the story of why we are selling our God Shot dream home. We are moving from our little town to the Boise area so that David and Paige can be in a church setting with more kids their age. We are seeing how important it is to feed their faith, to be part of giving them a God Shot by giving up our home. Orpha and I didn't necessarily want to move to Boise, but we know it is best for David to have a solid foundation to become a pastor.

Every child follows God in a unique way, just like every family creates its own unique story. We didn't just wake up one day ready to sell our home, nor did Paige just happen to sense God's timing for our family to move to Idaho. The Lord gives parents God Shots to nudge them closer to their child's unique heart. When we take time to show our kids who the Lord is and show our hearts for the special things that happen, we partner with God to give our children God Shots.

We are doing things differently than our parents did for us, and I want to share a few of our insights that work for our family. I want to share two verses of Scripture that are so meaningful when it comes to parenting.

"Start children off on the way they should go, and even when they are old, they will not turn from it." (Proverbs 22:6)

"Fathers, do not exasperate your children; instead, bring them up in the training and instruction of the Lord." (Ephesians 6:4)

I. THE PROPER ORDER OF PRIORITIES IS GOD, US, THEN KIDS

Major moves in our family came from the suggestion and needs of our kids. Remember Paige suggesting it was time to move to Idaho? Guess what? It was! Our latest move will support David and give him what he needs to be the best version of himself. It will also be in line with our priorities in life: 1) God; 2) Us (Orpha and I); 3) Our kids. In that order. So many families, including parents, are messed up because people have gotten those priorities mixed up.

The concept of "training up a child" means much more than giving rules, bedtimes, and a roof over your kids' heads. Raising kids is an all-in commitment, making us do things we would never consider without them.

Training your children in the ways of the Lord can be a blessing for you *and* them. Because Paige was sensitive to the leading of the Lord, we made the move to Idaho. However, the move has also blessed both Orpha and me. Supporting your kids is not just part of training your kids to help them not depart from the Lord. They are more likely not to depart from you, either.

Supporting your kids might require sacrifice, but it will always be a blessing. This move to Boise is a little bit of a delicate thing for us. We're not telling David we're sacrificing because we don't want him to carry a burden that is ours and not his. But wow, it has been a hard move. To be honest, it was best for us also. We are closer to our church community, closer to my and Dave's appointments, which are required several times per week, and closer to the things we need to do daily.

2. BEING INTENTIONAL KEEPS US FROM PROVOKING OUR KIDS

Dads, let's get real. We know a lot of ways to provoke our kids because we've all been emotionally provoked by our fathers. Most men can recall a time when their father did not listen to their side of a story and cut off a discussion. Some guys have different interests and skill sets from their dad, and he just didn't get it.

Other dads grew up without their fathers and have conflicted feelings about being a dad. Men also grow up with dads who are physically around but a million miles away, with their minds on work, hobbies, drugs, or the TV.

Most guys come pre-wired to find some way of provoking their children. If you think about a house, men's brains are like a long hallway connected to individual rooms. Men can close a door, lock it, and never even peek into the room again. We might even forget what's in that room! Because we can close doors, it's easy for us to live like our kids have the same door shut with the same bad stuff behind those doors.

One way we can keep from provoking our kids is to be intentional in how we spend time with them—making time for them forces us to look at our kids and what is going on in their lives, to open doors that might be closed off in our own minds.

Being intentional does not have to be complicated. Make simple plans that put your kids at the center of your time and attention. You can:

- Go to ball games
- Volunteer to be part of scouting, youth group, or school activities
- Go shopping, and look at stuff that brings a smile to your kid's face
- Do something outside together, like walking, hiking, boating, or shooting targets
- Read books together and enjoy stories

One last thought about feeling provoked. Do you recall ever doing things to get your parents to pay attention to you? Were you the jokester, storyteller, information sharer, TV remote hider, or loud one?

Our kids want our attention and need it. If you feel provoked, do a gut check. Is your kid saying, "Hey, Dad, I need some of your time?" If so, get intentional with something they like to do, and make a great life together!

3. EVERY SEED YOU PLANT COUNTS FOR SOMETHING

Orpha and I grew up in families that knew about God but did not experience Him together. Our parents celebrated Christmas and Easter with our families because "it was the thing to do," and our grandparents did it. I went to Sunday school class from time to time, but it never meant too much to me or my family.

We grew up around God and knew some stuff about God, but we didn't know God's character and certainly did not have a relationship with his son, Jesus Christ. It would not be a stretch to say our family Bible got more use from our golden retriever as a chew toy than anyone in our house reading it!

But here's the deal; even those little seeds of faith caused us to go to church in our thirties, forever changing our lives. We never know what seed will germinate in our kids' lives or when it will take off and grow. Take a look at these scriptures again:

"Start children off on the way they should go, and even when they are old, they will not turn from it." (Proverbs 22:6; emphasis mine)

"Fathers, do not exasperate your children; instead, bring them up in the training and instruction of the Lord." (Ephesians 6:4; emphasis mine)

Every farmer knows his harvest does not happen by accident. You may recall that I worked around produce, and I can tell you that almond and pistachio farmers do not just take a walk into a field on some random day and start harvesting the nuts. Farmers have to plan how they get and manage land, seeds, water, fertilizer, labor, shipping, and other variables.

Training, discipline, and instruction are faith seeds we can plan in our children's lives. Our job as parents is to plant seeds that can grow into faith.

Children have a part to play in the generational faith transfer, too. In Mark chapter 10, Jesus tells the story of a young man who wanted to follow Jesus. Jesus asked him if he had kept the commandments God gave to Moses. The young man said he had done so since birth, and then Jesus challenged him to go deeper. He told the young man to sell everything he owned, give it to the poor, and follow Him.

The young man went away sad. Why? Was it because he did not know God? No, his parents had taught him well. He went away sad because he chose to walk away from Jesus rather than sell the things he owned. The young man's parents did everything they knew to train, discipline, and instruct him. The faith seeds they planted in his soul drew him to Jesus. We don't know if this young man ever came to place faith in Jesus as Messiah or not, but we know his parents did their job.

They showed the young man enough about God to come face to face with Jesus. I'm praying with you that our kids can come face to face with Jesus because I know how much He loves them.

4. FAITH IS MORE CAUGHT THAN TAUGHT

"More caught than taught" is a popular saying about parenting because it is easy to remember, and it is true. Children learn more from the things they see and do than from a formal lesson. Toddlers learn to talk by repeating the words they hear from adults. We often joke about the habits "mini-me" get from their parents. They walk, talk, pronounce words, and tell jokes like Mom, Dad, and the other important adults in their lives.

The fact that children (and adults, for that matter) learn from our model should tell us how important it is to live our faith in God. Yes, our kids will see the big ways we trust God with a move, looking for a new job, or dealing with a crisis in the family. But they learn how to walk every day with Jesus, to have "blue jeans" Christianity from the way we honor God.

So, what is your model as a man or woman who follows Jesus Christ? Here are a few thoughts:

Money. Jesus gave a lot of attention to the subject of money. More than 33% of his parables talk about money. Money is not evil but is a tool for use in God's kingdom. Jesus spoke about how we make money, spend money, depend on God for money, and give money. What opportunities do your kids have to see you make decisions with money?

Time. Our real priorities in life are where we spend time and money. We make time for the things that are important to us. To put it another way, where we spend our time is important to us. What do your kids know about you from how you spend your time?

Prayer. The disciples asked Jesus to teach them to pray. Prayer, talking, and listening to God, is not our natural first language. Just like small children learn words and accents by repeating what they hear, we learn to pray by listening to others pray. How are you helping your kids become fluent in speaking to and hearing from Jesus?

Serving. You don't need a spiritual gifts test to serve in the Kingdom of God. In fact, the hard ways God might ask us to serve may go against everything we naturally want to do. We mentioned the young man who wanted to follow Jesus and how serving the poor became his stumbling block. Are your kids seeing you grow in service to the Lord or being busy with church activities?

The Fruit of the Spirit is love, joy, peace, patience, kindness, faithfulness, gentleness, and self-control. Each piece of fruit is a slice of character we put into our lives, which people can see. How do you rank in each of these areas?

Remember, your kids are modeling the same type of joy and self-control that you model. While each child has natural areas of weakness, it's worth our time to consider that a character weakness in our kids could come from our lack of modeling.

A WORD TO A FAMILY IN TRAUMA

My accident challenged every part of our family life, including our parenting. We are different people, different parents, and a different family after he sustained so many injuries. God has been so good to us and restored so much of Dave's health and life that we can't put all of it into words.

However, it has had an impact on our family, and it takes time in the right environment to receive healing. Physical therapy has taught us that healing is more than a single first step. Healing is a process that keeps going and growing for our minds, bodies, souls, and emotions to become whole. In some ways, we will always be healing in this world because it is full of sin and broken pieces.

Parenting is all about making an environment for our kids. So, if you have suffered through a difficult time as a parent, you have double-healing duty. Not only do you need to get well for yourself, but you have to get well for your kids. Once I saw a quote by Ayesha Siddiqi, "Be the adult you needed as a child." What a great reminder!

GOD SHOTS FOR SUCCESS

1. Do your kids know you have their back no matter what life throws at them? When they have problems, are they coming and talking with you, or do you find out after everyone else? Talk with your spouse about ways to support your kids and build their trust.

2. Dad, are you more intentional about provoking or providing love? Think through the last few interactions with your kids. Do both of you walk away happier and better? Is there more correcting than encouraging? Would you feel encouraged if your dad treated you like you are treating your son or daughter?

3. How are you sowing the seeds of the gospel? Going to church is great, but the Bible says that parents are the ones who are responsible for training, instructing, and disciplining their children. How do your kids look at God by looking at you? What does your fathering and mothering say about God's heart for kids?

4. Are you living the life you want your kids to catch? What do they see in the way you work and love your spouse? How are they involved in making time and money decisions within the family? Do you expect them to act like you, or is it "do what I say, not what I do?"

Chapter 10

WORK: BECOMING
THE LEADER PEOPLE NEED

BY DAVE

My career as an engineer started like many other professionals. I dressed in a suit and tie and went to work feeling like a little boy at a conference table filled with grown-ups. Every experience was new, and I observed a difference between managers and leaders.

I soaked in these lessons on visits, making reports to the executives at my first job. I remember it as a sterile environment with little personality or personal interaction. Desk after desk had the same look—a pad of paper and a pen. Each desk might have something unique; a coffee cup, a family photo, or a book. But for the most part, it all felt like work without life.

People did not interact with each other. Vice presidents did not talk to one another. When they did, it was like being called onto the mountain of the high and mighty. They acted with power but were separated from the people and everyday processes of the company. I was intimidated and felt scared to approach those guys.

It took me a while to learn that it had more to do with them than it did me.

All the vice presidents, except the one I modeled my career after, were part owners of the company. Arrogant is the word that sticks with me when I think about them. I saw too many people put in office time as a showpiece to collect millions of dollars without getting involved.

When people started reporting to me, I chose the path of a leader who is part of the life and processes of my company. I learned that loyalty cannot be forced or bought. Instead, it comes to those who protect their people.

LOYALTY AND TRUST

Loyalty and trust are two qualities that are indispensable for leadership. However, people do not automatically give them to you. You must earn them. They can never be demanded.

They are not part of a title, position, or job description. Some people will only look at a manager or executive as "the boss" who keeps them at arm's length. I focused my time and energy on people who accepted a positive impact on their lives. When I found those people, I made it my job to bring positive change and challenges, not punitive actions.

I made it a point to interact, to know, and be known by my staff. I had people dance with me on the spur of the moment at company barbeques and picnics. I got invitations to weekend cookouts and celebrations from so many of my direct reports. People would walk with me through the factory, the plant floor, and the business office, looking for some sort of interaction. And my workers were very loyal. They would follow me to the ends of the earth and always looked out for my best interests.

The lesson I learned early on is that loyalty is earned and not demanded by a dictator. A dictator-style leader always tries to get people to move where he wants them to go. The servant leader is in the front, pulling people along on the journey everyone wants to take!

This is not a new concept at all. In fact, Jesus himself talked about the best style of leadership in Matthew 20:25-28. He said this:

Jesus called them together and said, "You know that the rulers of the Gentiles lord it over them, and their high officials exercise authority over them. Not so with you. Instead, whoever wants to become great among you must be your servant, and whoever wants to be first must be your slave—just as the Son of Man did not come to be served, but to serve, and to give his life as a ransom for many."

In my professional life, I have always tried to model servant leadership. I have sometimes failed, as any leader does. But over the years, I've found that it is by far the best way to lead people and make an organization successful.

In the rest of this chapter, you'll learn several important aspects of servant leadership. If you practice these principles, you can make a positive impact and ensure loyalty from those you lead. We'll close this chapter with a few words of advice for new leaders.

PROBLEM-SOLVING

Problem-solving can and should be taught. I used to interview folks, and my first question was, "Tell me about a real-life problem you solved under time pressure?" I didn't want a contrived school assignment. Many gave good answers because they either grew up on a farm or were very hands-on with their work. Either way, they understood what and why I was asking.

I was not digging for the right words, technique, or reporting procedure. No, I wanted to understand their overall thought process. Problem-solving goes deeper than one solution for one issue. I wanted to know what people did when everything fell apart, and there were no clear-cut answers. Where did they go to get the necessary information? Who did they include and did not include in the solution? What happened when they failed?

I found these to be keys to problem-solving of all types. How we treat people and include them is important. When things are falling apart around you and your team, there is no room for ego, pride, or delusions of grandeur. Period!

When it's fixed, everyone is congratulated or even rewarded. Thinking outside the box and knowing where to go for new information is critical. We will all face failure in a real "this has to be fixed now" situation. How people deal with themselves, others, and work, makes a huge difference to team performance.

We could have wallpapered our offices with all the MBA charts and graphs of would-be consultants who were there to "help us get better." But problems in the production line, factory, and office are solved in the now and not in training sessions. I find it all a bit pathetic and funny. My real experts were the people working and living around me every single day. I found much, much more success with natural problem solvers than consultants.

In other words, train your people to solve problems, and they will help you solve the problems around you.

RESPECT AND DIGNITY

I want to emphasize the importance of having respect and dignity for everyone who works for you, no matter the situation. I learned that respect and humility will be paid back at least ten-x by the people you serve. That is what I miss the most about my early retirement. It's not the work or leading some 2,000 people to process millions of pounds of pistachios and almonds. What I really and truly miss is having the ability to impact lives for good.

The challenges associated with working alongside people and serving them are . . . well . . . challenging. I had real cultural challenges. A large portion of my workforce was Hispanic. I wish I'd learned more Spanish instead of the French I studied in high school. At least then, I would have known for sure if they were cursing at me!

Problem-solving exercises at the plant included people from all disciplines who could help brainstorm solutions to get to the root cause of the issues. I attended those sessions to make sure every person affected in the process could contribute.

For example, if we had a problem on a production line, we naturally had mechanics, engineers, production operators, and floor operators directly involved in the process. You have a wide range of experience and expertise, ranging from the hourly wage earner to engineers who could be arrogant. An engineer might jump right in saying, "I know what the problem is," and shut down everyone else while he went on and on about his point of view.

I'd make a point to go to those problem-solving sessions and be there as a friend. I showed my support for everyone as the leader. If someone got off track and the conversation shut down, I could quickly stop them and call up those who had their own two cents to share.

If an arrogant engineer said, "I know the department and the problem," I'd say, "Okay, that's good for you. Sit down now, and let's hear opinions from the other people here." I surprised a lot of people with long-winded explanations because I sat in the back watching. Usually, they wouldn't know I was there until I said something or they looked up.

I liked doing that stuff. I liked being part of the process. I loved being part of the interaction between the departments. I could hear my people in the plant, maintenance, or wherever, saying their two bits. It was a way for me to learn about people's strengths and weaknesses. I could see firsthand how they acted, reacted, and interacted as real human beings.

Everyone, all 2,000+ employees, knew they could be heard, and I enjoyed it. I enjoyed doing things that were not recorded. Those were the moments in meetings where loyalty and respect were earned. My place in the back of the room, piping up at the right time, made me an effective leader.

TAKING A DAILY WALK

I learned another servant leadership skill from Deryl, the one consultant who truly had tremendous amounts of problem-solving wisdom for us. Deryl was the retired president of Toyota North America, so he knew a thing or two about the subject.

I foolishly thought, originally, that to get the updates on the plant floor, I just needed to model my mornings like the owner or manager of a casino by getting a folder with the previous day's information. The folder tells him the profit and loss of the previous day, what's running well, and a summary of the problems. It's a snapshot of the last twenty-four hours for that business. Deryl helped set us straight.

I learned to begin my daily walk on the factory floors (called Gemba walks) through the plants at the main site near my office. Then I drove ten minutes north to another factory to walk the floor, moving from one plant to another, and then I drove back.

It was more important to be out and about with the folks in the plants. The best way to be there was by walking around from plant to plant. I learned how they ran the last twenty-four hours and what problems came up. I asked what problems they were working on, their successes, or if they had obstacles coming from other departments. I reviewed the results of their Gemba boards, which had the same general content plant to plant.

If it involved the quality departments, I would find out if they were putting production on hold, not getting feedback somewhere, and why it was happening. That was part of my morning routine every day.

FOLLOWING UP AND FOLLOWING THROUGH

If there was an obstacle with departments under other vice presidents, such as the quality control department or the purchasing department, I needed to get involved. When those types of issues came up for my departments, I first had to speak with a fellow vice president or someone on my side of influence.

I always volunteered and said, "Alright. I will take care of that." If they thought it was too big of a deal, I responded, "Hey, this is the problem we're dealing with. Were you aware of it?" Often, they said they did not know about it. So, we got the problem fixed, and my people recognized that we, including me, always found a way to fix problems.

Follow-up and follow-through for your people creates loyalty. When you stand up for your people, they notice. When you stand up with a problem they created because they were in the wrong, you want to make sure they own up to it. That's how the loyalty road runs.

But if your people have a roadblock that is out of their control, you need to break that roadblock and make sure it stays broken down and out of their way. Fixing a problem outside another person's control and making sure it does not crop up again also earns loyalty.

When you follow through and help your people fix a problem, don't make it a big deal. Too many managers and leaders want to thump their chests and say, "Look what I did. I just pulled this string and pushed those policies in the company." You need to do the right thing for the good of the people. After all, isn't that what you expect from them? To show up, do their job, solve problems when they arise and get the job done together?

If a problem is impeding the work of your people, then heaven knows it is probably impeding the work of a lot of other people. For the good of both your own department as well as everyone else, you want to solve that issue and solve it quickly.

For example, a manager once came to me with a problem related to microwaves. Our folks had a thirty-minute lunch break before they had to get back on the floor and get the production line moving. If people have a half an hour lunch, but half that time is spent waiting in line for a microwave, they've got to rush to get their meal, get it warmed up, and scarf it down. If they make it back in time, they probably won't expect your line back up and running on time. That creates a problem for the entire factory.

But if they can get to the microwave quickly and easily, they will get back to the lineup on time. So, we bought a bunch of microwaves, which solved the problem. Simple, but easy to miss. Everybody wins.

It's amazing what you hear by walking around the place where people work rather than sitting in your office. It's also amazing what happens when people trust you enough to bring you a simple but real problem rather than needing to go to a sterile executive suite.

SLOWING DOWN TO SPEED UP

I always picked people's brains and listened for any issue related to safety. When a cleaning crew member from the sanitation department talked about how long it took to clean something, sometimes I would have to say, "Sorry. I know this takes a long time, but there's no other way to do it. You've got to go slow and take your time to get through the work because it is important." Other times, I would say, "You know what, I think we can solve that hang-up."

Both responses involve slowing down to speed up. It's a process that takes extra time to perform but often keeps other parts of the process or the entire business moving efficiently.

One part has to move slowly so that everyone else can move fast. On the other hand, changing a process doesn't happen with the snap of the fingers. Everyone who is involved needs to fix the problem together. Again, we slow down to look at the issue from many sides and start moving faster once the thing is behind us.

That was my job as a leader. It's how I had to travel the loyalty road. Sometimes, you have to use other people's loyalty because there is no other way to do a job. Other times, you build their loyalty by going through a change process with them. In the end, we all have to trust each other's motives and actions to perform our best.

CULTIVATING HUMILITY

Rick Warren has said it well. "Humility is not thinking less of yourself; humility is thinking of yourself less." The key to being humble is focusing on the good of others and not worrying about the cost to yourself. Those are easy words to say, but they are a challenge to live at work, in marriage, or anywhere we connect with other people.

I'm no expert, but here are three small things that made a big difference in my leadership.

Pray for your people. I started praying every day for my team, asking how I could serve them. To pray and release God's power into the world and have Him partner with you at work is a blessing to you and everyone around you.

Put yourself aside. Early on, someone told me that to be an effective leader; you need to set yourself aside. You've got to get out of your mind, your own needs, and your comfort zone and step out and help people. I am thankful I learned that early; it has never been a huge struggle for me.

Know your filters. I do have a weakness here. I struggled to put myself aside when getting ideas from people I deemed arrogant or those who acted like they had a solution but didn't. I find it hard to take information from "the smartest guy in the room." The problem is that I could miss a potential solution from prideful people because of how I felt. All of us have some filter for getting along with others, and we need to name those filters and make sure they are working both for us and, when necessary, against us.

ADVICE FOR YOUNG LEADERS

Starting your work life can be a challenge. I've managed several thousand people and learned a few things over the years I would like to share with you. Getting started on the right foot can make a huge difference in your career.

Be a learner. We are all happy you have a college or high school education. Now, please, please remember . . . you still don't know everything. Put aside your old GPA, honors certificates, successes, and failures as a student. You are now in the workforce, and life begins anew.

Asking questions can teach you a lot of things about life and work. But understand this; how you ask questions tells everyone around you more about you. Ask questions as a learner. Don't be "that kid" who asks questions to make someone else look silly or to make themselves look good. We are smart enough to tell the difference.

Be a winner. Work to get the job done and make a win for everyone. In other words, if you work eight hours a day and always clock out at eight hours, everyone will assume you're just a clock puncher, and you're not in it to win it.

Make yourself into the model employee of your job, division, and company. Don't think everyone needs to change around you. Instead, you be the one to raise the expectations of others. Be willing to put in the time. Treat each piece of equipment and process in the factory as if you are an owner. Write and design as an owner and someone who will need to maintain and build on your work today.

Own your career. When problems and solutions come up, own it. If you have direct influence, jump in, and get things fixed. If you cannot directly control the problem, find the root of the problem, and find a solution. Don't wait for someone to make your work life better. Own it, fix it, and make it better. People will notice, and you will enjoy your work because it is yours.

Go all in. That's also part of owning your job. Don't be a clock puncher pretending to be a leader. Don't be a clock watcher. Be a leader. People are watching.

GOD SHOTS FOR SUCCESS

1. Jesus was a leader who made other leaders willing to die for a vision. The results of Jesus's style of leadership, of being a string-puller, not a string pusher, are still growing today. What examples do you have of leaders who push and leaders who pull? Are you following up and following through to build trust as a leader?

2. Opportunities are problems turned upside down from a frown into a smile. People wanted a product, pistachios, and it was our job to give it to them. My team wanted to make a living and make a difference, and we found ways to do that together. How do you engage problems? Are you talking with God and seeing what He sees? Do you exercise humility with your people during problem-solving times?

3. Servants lead, and dictators push. Which do you like working for and with? Review the suggestions for growing in humility. Which one do you need to work on right now? Ask God to give you a shot of grace so that you can be a God Shot to your team.

Chapter 11

PROTECTION: STANDING UP FOR OTHERS

BY DAVE

A be, whom you met in Part 1 of this book, worked in the office next to me for several years. He's a good guy, a very smart and motivated individual. He grew up with his brother in *very* tough neighborhoods in the inner city near Los Angeles, California.

Abe shared stories about growing up that involved violence and guns. He had a plan and dedicated himself to school and wrestling, excelling at both. He was always trying to better himself and loved learning. He took classes at universities to keep growing. Abe also loved his family.

As I said, he's a great guy. But great guys can also have really bad days. One day at work, I noticed that Abe just wasn't being Abe. He's a natural loud talker, and since my office was next door to his, I was used to hearing his conversations.

I didn't mean to eavesdrop, but he was on the phone, and this time Abe was really loud and wasn't sounding normal. My spirit was uneasy, but I shook it off and refocused at my desk. I gathered all my notes and got ready to take my walk through the factory. I turned back and saw Abe.

His office was in the corner, and when I looked back down the hall through his open door, he was sitting at his desk, and I knew something was wrong. I'm not sure if it was the Holy Spirit grabbing my attention, his body language, or both, but I knew I needed to speak to him right then. I made a loop back to the areas where our offices were, stepped into his office, and closed the door behind me.

"Abe, man, what's wrong?"

He was a wreck. His eyes were bloodshot, and his nose was running. I knew he had been crying.

I found out over the next several minutes that Abe's life as he knew it was falling apart. His wife, the center of the family he loved so much, had reconnected with a former boyfriend on Facebook. Messages turned to phone calls, and one thing led to another. She was divorcing Abe and leaving him for her former boyfriend.

"Abe, can I sit down?"

While listening, my mind was flooded with a ton of thoughts. I knew Abe loved his family. My mind flashed back to when I gave up my turn using the company condo in Hawaii. We had other plans and couldn't use it, so I asked if he wanted to take our time slot. I remember that he went with his wife and son. I didn't know his family well at the time, but he told me things that revealed a lot about his heart.

We talked, and I prayed with him for a while. We must have talked and prayed for over an hour because a shift change happened when I was ready to do my factory walk. I don't remember everything I said or specific things I prayed for. But I know I prayed for him, his wife, and his son that God would get them through.

I stood up, shook his hand, and said, "Abe, you're going to be fine. You'll get through this, man. You'll get through this."

What I didn't know was that Abe was planning to go home and shoot himself. He had a gun loaded, cleaned, oiled, and ready to do the job. It was at home on his counter waiting for him. His plan before, and especially after, that loud phone call was to go home and end it all. He thought he had found a permanent solution to a temporary problem by committing suicide.

I had no idea of the thoughts and despair dancing in his mind when I sat down to talk and pray with him. But later on, after my accident, he confided this little tidbit to me. None of us knows what might or might not have happened if I had not stopped to pray with him. He just might have found that permanent solution.

WE SAVED EACH OTHER'S LIVES

God began to work things out for Abe, and today, he is doing great. He is a fantastic dad who loves his son and loves doing all kinds of things with him. Abe and his son live together, and they get a chance to go places and do all sorts of things together.

Abe was at a nearby filling station and market on the day of my accident. He's the one who heard the collision. I suppose he was there because I needed some help. I was told later that he had been preparing for a big-budget review the following day. Abe was great with numbers. Our budgets could get complicated with seasonal crop projections and other variables, but Abe loved analyzing data. He's a professional analyst and has built models used by colleges. I had wanted him to look at my budget and help me with the report.

Abe had an intern working with him that year. They left the world of numbers for a few minutes to refuel and refocus their bodies with ice cream and something to drink. The market is at the intersection of Highway 36 and Highway 44, just a couple of miles from the factory. If I hadn't asked for his help and their need to refuel for some late hours of number crunching, this would be a different story.

But Abe was there, and when he heard the crash, he called emergency services at the factory and got everyone moving to come and save me. The quick response of my rescuers was the difference between me sharing this awesome God Shot story of my life and being dead.

Abe's quick actions saved my life that day. The God Shots of this story are all over the place, aren't they?

Abe's life and my life could have been very different if I had not stopped to talk and pray with him.

I needed Abe's help on a report, which led to a snack run, and that saved my life.

Abe's quick thinking got the ball rolling, saving every second I needed to live.

I believe, with all my heart, that God kept Abe around to save my life right when I was a part of saving his. Why? I have no idea. But the Lord had mercy on me; therefore, I dedicate my life to serving Him and growing His Kingdom.

One interesting side note to this story; the market where Abe stopped was the last place James Dean stopped before he died crashing his Porsche 990 Spyder. The store's name? "James Dean's Last Stop."

Fortunately, the day of my accident was not my *last stop*!

SARAH ANNE'S STORY

Sarah Anne was our second child and holds a special place in a long list of God Shots. Through Sarah Anne, God changed our lives and helped us love life even more.

Orpha had a routine OB appointment in Bakersfield, about an hour from my office. I felt God telling me to show up at the OB's office, so about an hour before; I told my boss, "I'm taking the rest of the day off."

I arrived just as Orpha was taken back for her ultrasound. The ultrasound technicians are not supposed to say anything about what they see in order to let the doctor share the news. Technicians are human too, and we could see the very worried expression on the face of the one who was working with us.

Our tech talked with the doctor, and they gave us the news. Sarah Anne's body was not forming in a normal way. We thought maybe she had a clubbed foot or was missing a limb. Orpha's doctor and the tech did not say much but helped us schedule a 3-D ultrasound at Cedar Sinai in Los Angeles.

3-D ultrasounds make an awesome, life-like video of your baby. During our appointment at Cedar Sinai, we could see that Sarah Anne did not have a clubbed foot or a missing leg. Her whole body was deformed by thanatophoric dysplasia (TD).

TD is a kind of dwarfism that occurs in 1 in 25,000-50,000 newborns. We knew before Sarah Ann was born that her odds of living were zero. TD symptoms include an enlarged head, elongated fingers, extremely brittle bones, and a tiny rib cage which causes the child to struggle for oxygen.

The OB geneticist told us they could "take care of it for us." I asked her what she meant, and she nonchalantly replied, "an abortion."

In shock, I think I blurted out, "No! God's the author of life and death!"

The geneticist replied in a matter-of-fact tone "Dead is dead. It does not matter if she lives five minutes or fifteen."

We do not believe in abortion. It's important to just take pregnancies from incest and rape off the table when debating this topic. Less than 2% of abortions come from rape and incest so please, let's just take that argument off the discussion block. Our view on abortion informed how we dealt with this situation.

Sarah Anne was born via c-section. I can tell you, as I write this through tears, which are unusual and amazing coming from me, that I can still see Sarah Anne's beautiful blue eyes look up at me right after the doctor handed her to me. I've never seen or held a prettier, more special, or more blessed baby than Sarah Anne.

Sarah Anne never knew it (and that OB geneticist never knew it either), but her birth and short life changed people's lives. People placed their faith in Christ because of her short four-day life outside Orpha's womb.

You should have seen her funeral. The outside service was packed because of our little girl. I wrote a eulogy, a letter to Sarah Anne. You can read it in the appendix.

When Sarah Anne was fighting for her life, I prayed a lie. It might have happened on Day 2, or maybe it was Day 3—they blend together. I prayed for God to snatch up his little Sarah angel and take her back home. I know this is normal for parents facing the death of a child—for God to take them home and spare them pain.

But I did not pray for her sake as I told myself. No, I was not focused on the relief of all pain she might be in, but she wasn't in any. I prayed for Sarah Anne to leave for the sake of her Mommy and me. We'd been up several days with zero sleep. So, I lied . . . lied to myself, lied to my wife, and I lied to God.

But God knew my confused, broken, battered, and tired heart. Thank you, Lord, for trusting us with that precious little darling.

WHAT I LEARNED FROM JERRY

Here's another story about the value of life and why we must protect it. But this one is much more light-hearted!

In sixth grade, the "city powers-that-be" decided to desegregate Seattle schools. I played a part in their interests in that. I rode the bus across the city every single school day with the rest of my 6th-grade class.

We attended Madrona Elementary School—a predominantly black school. My best friend, Jerry, was a black kid that lived across the street from me in 4th and 5th grade. Jerry's dad was in the Navy, and they moved around a lot.

One day, we were playing in a tree in front of his house and saw a group of white kids strolling down the street. These white kids started yelling all kinds of racial garbage at us. Before I understood what was being said, and much more before I could move, Jerry jumped out of the tree and took off after those kids.

By the time I caught up to him, he already had one of the boys laid out on the ground and was ready to dish out more justice to the other kids. I thought (and still think) it was awesome! Those kids never had an issue with Jerry again.

WHAT IT MEANS TO BE A GENTLEMAN

I have a vivid memory of a time when Dad and I were at a department store in Salem, Oregon. I was twelve or thirteen years old and was out shopping with Dad when I saw a clerk berated by a man. This guy had lost his mind and was going off on this poor gal. He kept hollering and making a scene while this lady tried to explain her situation and fight back the tears from the verbal assault.

Even at a young age, I knew this was not good. I knew this was not how to treat anyone, especially a woman. I kept looking for the shop manager to jump in and stop this maniac. He wasn't around, so I looked at my dad and wondered, *Hey, when are you going to step in and defend this lady?*

He never did. It left a profound mark on me that helped shape my beliefs, including my disgust for bullies.

Men, we need to be gentlemen. I believe being a gentleman is required for all men at all times. I do not believe it's okay to act out of anger, even righteous anger, towards others. But God has made us to protect one another and that goes double for men.

We need to protect the weak. Men, look around and notice children, the disabled, the elderly, and others who need help. That is part of what it means to be a gentleman. We must notice people and act.

We also need to protect those who are less capable of protecting themselves. God calls us to protect women. Look, I don't think women are less capable than men in many things. But the plain and simple truth is that we are physically different. God made us to complement one another. Both men and women are made in God's image, and together we show what God is like. Men, we have to do our part.

Dads, this also means we need to teach our sons, their friends, and other young men what it means to be a gentleman.

WE MUST SPEAK UP

Speak up. That is what it means to be a gentleman. A man's physical presence does not require violence with either his body or his words when defending the weak.

In fact, Jesus gives us a much different point of view in the Sermon on the Mount and, specifically, the Beatitudes. Have you ever heard, "Blessed are the meek," "Blessed are the peacemakers," or "Blessed are the persecuted?" Our speaking up must fit Jesus's commands to his kingdom people.

The way of Jesus is the way of love, and love means we need to speak up for the discriminated, weak, abused, and others being manipulated and controlled.

You can speak with love. In love, you can tell an angry man berating a clerk, "Hey, calm down now. She's trying to do her job—

can you see what she's trying to do for you? Do you realize this is the way you're sounding? Do you realize that if this happened to you, you would be upset, and you would be doing the same thing this clerk is doing?"

Speaking for protection comes from a place of love and understanding, not a place of hate and anger. You might be like me and find your raw nerves getting stepped on when you see a bad situation. I find it hard to calm down, but with prayer, patience, and practice, we can all notice others and speak on their behalf.

The Christian community needs to step up, step out, and speak loud and clear for those struggling. I know I wanted to see it happen in that department store. I wish my dad had said something. I wish we would all protect one another.

CHRISTIANS AND SOCIAL JUSTICE

One of the most important ways to be Christ's hands and feet is to protect people from evil. The Apostle Peter talks about how we are a group of high priests constantly interceding for one another and the world. In 1 Peter 2:9-10, he says, "But you are a chosen people, a royal priesthood, a holy nation, God's special possession, that you may declare the praises of him who called you out of darkness into his wonderful light. Once you were not a people, but now you are the people of God; once you had not received mercy, but now you have received mercy."

God has made us a community to stand against the darkness, even when those trapped in darkness do not understand how we serve and love them. Christians ought to be the sheepdogs of the world, watching and protecting a vulnerable flock from wolves who would rip them to pieces.

Too many sheep think it's okay not to be armed. And yes, I mean with guns and other weapons. From their point of view, it's okay to live in a place that doesn't allow weapons, and, let's face it; they are not going to use a gun because they are sheep. They want to be in a safe pasture, and many people are happy to live in a place that wants to control their every move.

And life is fine . . . until it's not.

We protectors, the sheepdogs, need to be educated and equipped to protect ourselves and everyone around us. Our identity lies in dealing with any and every type of threat, no matter the source. That means being realistic about the pitfalls in life and having plans, ideas, and tools to deal with any and every problem.

That leads us to the abortion issue. God calls us to protect the widows and the orphans (James 1:27). What about the children who do not even have the chance to become orphans? Who will speak for them? Who will protect them from evil? Who will be the one to harm their unique DNA and rob them of the opportunity to love and be loved?

In 2022 as I'm writing this, racial issues are tearing up American life. Extremists from both ends and many points in between are making a lot of noise. The Bible makes it clear that the church, God's Kingdom, is not based on racial identity. Paul says in Galatians 3:28 that "There is neither Jew nor Gentile, neither slave nor free, nor is there male and female, for you are all one in Christ Jesus."

Believers need to think for themselves, be ready to speak in love, and listen in love in all situations. Too many people simply say what they hear on a newscast or read on the internet instead of using their powers of discernment and judgment.

As believers, we are for everyone, especially those that do not have a voice. More than anything, we are not "anti" anybody. We are for blacks, whites, Hispanics, and every other person and culture God has created.

Darkness prevails in so many places and hearts, yet Jesus calls us to be the "light of the world." Being light means we must love in words and deeds. Light protects and shields those who are weak. Light and love drive out darkness and hate.

FATHERS MUST PROTECT LIFE

Think of how many books, apps, conferences, websites, and other resources you have seen related to parenting. There are so many resources on parenting out there you can get lost in the information jungle without trying.

God has taught me a few things about parenting and protecting your family that probably run counter to a lot of that information. Here are my best suggestions:

Be present. The first thing is to be present in your family members' lives. A father needs to know what's going on with his wife, daughters, and sons. A father who does not know his family and who does not know what is happening cannot serve and protect in his unique role.

Show love and respect. Protection comes from an attitude and motive of love and respect. A very practical way to show respect is allowing everyone to be and grow into their unique human being. We must respect their decisions and the right to make decisions. We must respect their voice and the right to speak their minds. We must respect their desires and the right to dream and experience life.

Ask for help and advice. Right now, I'm a fifty-three-year-old male who grew up in an era without computers or cell phones. I am older than MTV! Oh, and did I mention I have brain trauma? So sometimes, I need help with a phone or an app. Every time I ask for help from my kids, it builds rapport and respect between us. And my phone works!

Be vigilant. Fathers, you need to protect your kids, your people, and your family from physical violence. I've mentioned that it is important to bear arms and be ready to protect our families. Fathers, our protection is part of the provision we must give our families.

I also teach my son, David, to be vigilant. We talk about how to deal with bullies who come after him and others. We plan what he can do and expect from Orpha and me if he encounters violence. He knows that it's best to try to stay out of the way when violence breaks out but also to be ready to defend himself.

David knows not to be the one to provoke or throw the first punch, and also to leave a bad situation and seek out authorities who can help. I'm preparing him to be light in the world, to watch out for himself and others, and to take care of his family in the future.

David is only in sixth grade as I sit and write this chapter. His world is so much different than the one I grew up in forty years ago. His high school experience will be another point of education for both of us.

Be a communicator. Love, respect, protection, vigilance, and all the rest depend on communication. I can't know what is going on in Paige, David, and Orpha's lives if we never communicate. We do a lot of our communication around the dinner table.

We have found dinner to be a very good time to hear how each other's days went, what's going on, and the plans we're all making. Dinner is a chance to catch a glimpse into their lives. Orpha and I can note if there's a problem and catch up with David or Paige later. Or maybe we will start intentional conversations about a problem area we see just over our meal.

I'm so glad I have a communications team with Orpha. Sometimes, she's ready to find out what is bothering one of the kids. Other times, I can play detective and see if we can get them to open up a little more.

Don't wait. Be a proactive communicator. I've learned at work and home that it's best to follow up on a question or idea quickly. Don't lose the moment. Even if your child does not choose to talk, they will remember that you stopped everything and made sure they were doing okay.

Fathers, we must get good at picking up clues from our families. We need to be experts at getting close and at giving and receiving love and respect from our families.

Be a prayer warrior. We also pray often. Every morning, Orpha and I start the day on our knees. Praying together in the morning helps me manage my emotions and all the other TBI fallout. We both notice that when we pray, I have good days, and when I skip prayer times for too long, life is not so good.

Let me put it this way; if we were not praying together, we would not be a married couple.

My brain is that messed up. I've seen the charts and graphs that explain traumatic brain injuries and how it affects brain function. The brain is so fascinating and complicated and can heal itself of many types of trauma. When you note the differences between mild, medium, and severe TBI, it's a steep and dramatic curve. The severity of the injury correlates with how long you were asleep after the injury, and I was out for a month. Even upon waking a month later, just a ten- to twelve-hour difference can bump someone from mild to medium to severe.

I bring all that up because my injury is real. Prayer is a real tool God has given me to use to fight for the life I need to live for myself and my family. But you don't need a brain injury to need a life of prayer. Jesus taught us in Matthew 6 how to pray and showed how life is different for us, our family, and others for whom we pray.

Prayer is a serious form of protection, and I'm so grateful God gives us a gift that blesses so many so well. It also blesses me in the process.

I've had to learn to pray again. I pray with my pastor and my friend, Lance. We can talk and pray about challenges in life. You see, Lance has ALS (Lou Gehrig's disease), and we both know what it is like to lose abilities and become handicapped. We are blessed to share our prayer lives.

Prayer is also a way I can do self-care. The last seven years have been a challenge for Orpha, and I'm sure I don't know half of what she has gone through. But now, I can share things with her that I need her to pray over, and she can share with me. Then I can go pray with my friends, and it's not all on her to be with me. So, we pray for each other all the time, and God blesses us through the protective grace of prayer.

You don't have to protect others alone. When you fight for others, God is fighting, blessing, and protecting right there alongside you.

GOD SHOTS FOR SUCCESS

1. God nudged me to speak with Abe when he was having one of the worst days of his life. How has God used you to speak to others? Has he nudged you, and you put Him off, or went "too late?" Make a commitment to notice people and notice God's promptings.

2. Sarah Anne was a blessing to us the world may never understand. God protected us in a time of deep trouble and taught us that no life should be abandoned. How do you value life inside and outside a mother's womb? What can you do to celebrate life?

3. How are you crossing racial and cultural boundaries to show care and love? Who are you speaking for? Men, how are you speaking up for women? And women, in a time when men are getting attacked, how are you speaking up for them?

4. Prayer is holding my life and marriage together. Every act of protecting my family is an act of prayer. How are you communicating with your spouse and kids? Do you know what they are thinking and doing?

Chapter 12

DANGERS:
RECOGNIZING THE WARNING SIGNS

BY DAVE

Have you ever been driving down the highway, lost in the nice weather or the music on the radio, and missed your exit? It's easy to do. When you are lost in the moment and aren't paying attention, you can completely miss the giant signs on the side of the road or suspended over your head.

Those signs give us key pieces of information for our journey. They tell us the distance to towns and exits, speed limits, dangerous curves, when to stop at an intersection, and more. Drivers who ignore the obvious signs on the road are a danger to themselves, other drivers, and pedestrians.

The physical signs posted along the highways are not the only ones we must pay attention to. Life is also constantly sending us warning signs. I've ignored those warning signs, and the price has been a lot of pain to my family and me. In truth, my choices to ignore clear warning signs have been almost as painful as the injuries caused by my accident.

Maybe you can relate.

One of the constant themes of the Bible is that God calls His people back to Himself time and again. In the Old Testament, God used the prophet Jeremiah to show them how they kept choosing the wrong way when He had made it so clear how to live.

My people have committed two sins:
They have forsaken me,
*   the spring of living water,*
and have dug their own cisterns,
*   broken cisterns that cannot hold water.* (Jeremiah 2:13)

Just like the people of ancient Israel, I have forsaken the living water of the Lord and made my own broken water tanks that left me dry. In this chapter, I'll share four specific areas where I have ignored the warning signs and paid the price. The warning signs are there for a reason—to guide us, help us, and save us. We ignore them at our peril.

I share these stories for two reasons. First, to remind you that God's ways are the best. I know the signs look like God is trying to take away fun and pleasure. But trust me, He is giving you boundaries that bring lasting joy.

Second, I want to remind you to choose God's tried and true ways. We always have the option of obeying or not obeying. Just like the prodigal son, we can get on the road that takes us home.

While I've paid a heavy price for my actions, I can tell you with all honesty that God's ways are the best ways. When you pay attention to the warning signs, you can avoid a lot of the problems that cause people to crash and burn.

WARNING SIGN #1: NOT INVESTING YOUR TIME WELL

Wealth and riches are best measured in time. The same experience can be called rich or poor, depending on our needs and focus. For example, an extra hour at work to make enough money for a long-desired family vacation can make you feel rich. The same hour of work spent to make enough money to pay a tax bill for a deadbeat family member can make you feel poor and bitter.

Your time budget, along with your financial budget, shows your real priorities in life. God does not pull punches on these kinds of things. The warning signs are clearly marked with His Way or the world's way. Just like Jesus saw through the words of the rich young man and made him put his money where his mouth was (Mark 10:17-31), God makes us stand at the crossroads and shows us where we spend our time.

Relationship budgets are first measured in time. Money is secondary. I know . . . our American culture screams that people want and need things to be happy. The fact is that poor people can be happier than rich people when they have a supportive community of people in their life. In an earlier chapter, I talked about going on mission trips to Central and South America, where I've seen very happy and content folks sweeping their dirt floors. They were proud of their families and relationships with their heavenly Father!

Let me cut to the chase. I spent time chasing my own hobbies and desires more than spending time with my family. My accident made me realize just how fragile my family life had become. I was blind and oblivious before my accident woke me up to reality.

I thought I was doing really well. I'd given up drinking and going to social events in mixed company. I was hiking, hunting, shooting, camping, and diving with buddies. I had my family and career. I was enjoying life.

But I had no idea how bankrupt I was.

My time budget created a steel wedge in my marriage. While I was out doing all the fun stuff there is to do in the Sierra Mountains, Orpha was left alone to raise the kids. I left all school activities, the important conversations with our daughter and son, and all the appointments—I left all of it to her.

The wreck was a wake-up call I desperately needed. Now that I am around all the time, I see the strain caused by all my time working and playing. Injuries make it hard for me to relate. Anger is ready to erupt at a moment's notice. God stuck me at a crossroads to make me deal with reality.

The past hurts, and my angry outbursts were causing a lot of problems between Orpha and me. She did not want to make the one-hour drive to church in Boise with me. Yeah, it was that bad. God made it clear I needed to change how I used my time with my family. I had to decide how to spend these next years of my life in a positive way.

Spending time is a lot of work. For those of you with a job, I know it can be tough to win at it, but we can't lose at home! Yes, we all need time to enjoy life, but don't let hobbies rob you of a family.

Making relationship investments is like making deposits into a bank account. We make positive deposits by speaking another person's love language and freely giving our time, affection, words, service, and gifts. We also make withdrawals by using hurtful words, spending time away from each other, working too much, or making other mistakes. These are things that draw people apart.

Here are a few thoughts on making practical investments of time.

1. **Put deposits toward your own team.** Spending more time at work gives us access to relationships with the opposite sex. I know the grass looks greener on the other side of the fence, but it still requires mowing. Where you spend time caring and putting your time—that's where the greenest grass grows. Instead of flirting with someone who is not your spouse, find ways to make your spouse feel special with the time and compliments you could give another person.

   You and your spouse are a team. Invest in each other, your family, and your future. Put your deposits into your own team, not with someone from the outside, with flirting, time, and attention. When your team falls apart, you will become cohabitators, distant roommates who barely know each other.

2. **You can do it, even when you have extra burdens.** For older people and injured people like me, relationships still take time. We know that we need extra help and care, but we also need to make deposits into our loved ones' lives. And we can do it!

   I put in extra time researching and getting good treatments, prayer, exercise, and more, focusing on being a better husband and dad. My injuries can make moments hard to handle. I have to work hard to manage those moments.

3. **Deposits bring more deposits.** Check your motives on how relationships work. *Manipulators* make a relationship deposit expecting a certain type of return from the other person. *Enablers* make deposits feeling like nobody should take care of them.

   Healthy people in a relationship built on honesty, trust, and respect do not go bankrupt making endless deposits into their spouse. They build a rich relationship by adding, building, and multiplying the deposits they make into each other.

4. **Don't rob from your family.** Making deposits of attention outside of your marriage and family rob them of what is rightfully theirs. Let me say that again; when you make deposits of time and attention outside of your wife and kids, you are robbing them. You are the one who controls how you spend your time. Do your kids and spouse feel robbed or rich?

   Time is a crossroads for all of us. Talk to the Lord and ask for His help in building those critical family relationships.

WARNING SIGN #2: NOT BEING FULLY PRESENT WITH YOUR FAMILY

How you show up in your family is just as important as being there. "Debbie Downers" are real! Certain people enter a chit-chat among friends, and suddenly, everyone is uncomfortable.

Kids especially know if you want to be with them or somewhere else. When they want more of your attention, they will do all kinds of things, from asking questions to throwing good old-fashioned temper tantrums. Kids also avoid people who are dangerous or make them uncomfortable.

Human survival depends on what we perceive in others. Fight or flight mode automatically kicks in when we are around people who feel like a threat. The people in our families notice what is happening inside of us.

Here are a few things I've noticed that keep us from being fully present.

1. **Work pressure.** "Keep it at the office" is easier said than done. Bringing the deadline and headaches of the job home is not fair to our families. They can't do anything about it, and the frustrations, anger, disappointments, and letdowns are not their fault. Leave your work at work and be present with your family.

2. **Anger and unmanaged feelings.** Bubbling over with joy can be great! Bubbling over with depression, anger, jealousy, envy, anxiety, and the like is terrible. Feelings are important and teach us something about ourselves and our situations. But, it's selfish when they go unchecked and spill out into family life and cause others to pick up pieces of your life,.

3. **Takers and sponges.** Some people take more from life, relationships, and work than they give. Not all of them mean to, and there can be reasons. The fact remains that people, including your family, avoid sponges. They are never satisfied.

4. **Physical pain.** Oh, how I know this is true! Pain can keep us out of our right mind. Sometimes the pain can get the best of us; we have short fuses, and our tempers can flare. While that is natural and understandable, it also keeps us from being present with people the way we want. On the other side of the coin, focusing on pain management can keep us from living with the people around us.

5. **Phones and media.** No list like this in the 21st century is complete without saying, "Put your phone down!" And books, streaming video, music, surfing the internet, and your other favorite media escapes. Be present, and not just around the house.

6. **Hobbies.** I mentioned earlier that even healthy hobbies can be destructive when they compete for time. We can spend more time thinking about fly-fishing, canoeing, hiking, and the like than having a chat with our kids who are at the other end of the couch.

God promises that we can overcome. The prodigal son in Luke 15:11-32 trusted that his father would at least give him a job as a slave. The father blew away his expectations. As he ran down the road, he threw his arms around him and called him "son." The rest of the story tells us there were still problems in the house. Not everything magically changed overnight.

God gives us grace to make the right choices at every point in our lives. Don't be fooled; we still have work to do! I've noticed a few things that are important parts of my work in being present. The good news, especially for men, is that there are practical steps to improve our relationships.

1. **Self-awareness.** The ancient Greeks inscribed "Know thyself" on Apollo's temple in Delphi. Paul says in Galatians 6:7, "Do not be deceived: God cannot be mocked. A man reaps what he sows." We are responsible for knowing what we are doing, thinking, saying, and how we behave.

2. **Tone of voice.** How you say something is part of the meaning. Hearing, "Oh, that's fine" from your loving, kind-hearted grandmother is different from, "Oh, that's fine," breathed out in frustration with an eye roll and cold shoulder.

3. **Posture and body language.** Speaking of eye rolls and cold shoulders, our bodies carry communication. When you "bristle with anger," people know it. My face does not express emotion. I just look mad or preoccupied all the time. My therapist pointed out how important this was in returning to work. People read us through our faces more than we know.

4. **Being pleasant.** Manners matter in how we are present. When your mind is engaged in pleasant thoughts and looking for ways to make positive connections, your communication is much better.

5. **Listening.** Steven Covey's influential book *The 7 Habits of Highly Effective People* made this the #5 Habit; "Seek First to Understand, Then Be Understood." When you have con-

versations, you will grow when you enter as a learner ready to become an expert on each member of your family.

6. **Communication.** Families face all sorts of challenges and demands for time, attention, and money. Nothing is more important than communicating with each other. Put it on a to-do list and make it happen.

7. **Prayer.** Connecting with God changes us and changes the world. The Lord makes an incredible offer from Jesus at every moment; I will partner with you to live life. Prayer is partnering with God. So why not let God teach you how to be present with others? Jesus is the universal expert on being with people!

WARNING SIGN #3: ADDICTION AND SUBSTANCE ABUSE

My sobriety date is February 18, 2010. I am an alcoholic, speaking from firsthand experience. I suppose I learned how to drink from my dad. My mom was a practicing alcoholic but stopped drinking after she divorced my dad. I grew up in Oregon with my dad and never witnessed someone stop drinking.

My dad was always busy and distant. Needless to say, we weren't close. Dad never drank during the day, and drinking never affected his job. He worked hard and then drank hard. He would let the vodka flow in the evenings, and he could drink up to half a gallon every weekend! Later in life, he stopped drinking, cold turkey, and as far as I knew, he never had another drink once he'd made up his mind to stop!

I started drinking cheap tequila in my senior year of high school. I never drank during the football season–that was far too important to screw up.

I became a professional drinker as a mechanical engineering student at Oregon State University. I pledged to the Theta Chi fraternity, and that rocketed my drinking. I started off just drinking on the weekends after classes were finished on Friday. Pretty soon, I was popping open my first can on Wednesdays. Soon, this high school valedictorian was flunking out of college. Thankfully, I got my act together enough to graduate, but alcohol was a big part of my college career.

Alcohol was part of my work culture, too. We never ever drank on the job, but after we punched out for the day, we drank. Several of us would get together and have drinks right after work. Employees had weekend parties where the alcohol flowed. Overnight business trips always included drinking.

I was a practicing alcoholic into my late thirties. While I managed not to drink on the job, I was still a walking time bomb. After walking through the plant, it was normal for my blood pressure to measure 200 over 100!

My drinking led me to a very dark place. A place of "*pitiful and incomprehensible demoralization,*" as AA's Big Book states it. I wanted to stop—but I could not stop. All my "want to's" and sincere earnestness was not enough. I couldn't quit!

One night, I got into a car wreck and was cited with a DUI. I had promised my wife and then young daughter I'd take them to a movie at 3:00 p.m. I never made it home. Instead of going to the movie with my girls, I planned the usual off-site meeting with my staff, which always led to having drinks after we finished. Even after the accident, which was clearly my fault, and all the praying and promising to God and Orpha that I would stop, I could not.

Here is a God Shot that came through a broken air conditioner.

Orpha called an AC company to repair our unit. The owner himself came out, and as he worked, he looked around our house. When he saw the overabundance of wine, beer, and hard liquor, he said, "Who's the drinker?"

Orpha replied, "My husband, Dave."

He gave Orpha his card and said, "Have him call me. I can take him to a meeting." He was in AA. Alcoholics Anonymous was my salvation! He introduced me to Bakersfield AA, where I'd eventually find a sponsor, get sober, and get some time under my belt before the accident.

AA saved my life and my marriage. Without AA, I would be divorced, and my kids would not live with their father. I'm pretty sure I would have died early from a car wreck, stroke, or some other alcohol problem. AA is the real deal.

I had the normal alcoholic problems:

I needed drinks before I saw people

I felt like leaving a glass of wine half empty was an abuse

I felt like the world was against me

I was always chasing that mystical place called "just there"

I didn't care if I took one drink or twenty. I was chasing that mystical place I went to when I was drunk. That became the place I lived for.

Living like you are alone on an island is the worst. I thought the world was out to get me, but really, I was making mistakes and screwing up my life. Everybody else stayed away just to keep from being sucked into the middle of my drunken whirlpool.

Paul says, in Ephesians 5:18, "Do not get drunk on wine, which leads to debauchery. Instead, be filled with the Spirit . . ." I am so much happier now that I am sober! Giving up the chase for that mystical place with alcohol is nothing compared to living my life present with the Lord, my wife, and my kids.

I was scared to death that I'd take that first drink now that I'd survived the accident with a TBI (Traumatic Brain Injury). I've read story after story of how TBIs lead to relapse and divorce. Some people that have brain injuries start drinking as soon as they can. The brain forgets how to fight addiction. After a person comes out of a coma or whatever injury they have suffered, they go back on the bottle.

God, working through Orpha's prayers and love, as well as a pretty solid foundation in AA, spared me from a return to alcohol.

WARNING SIGN #4: BITTERNESS TOWARD THOSE WHO HAVE HURT YOU

I was blindsided by a truck—literally! And it changed the course of my life. My body and brain now have broken pieces I must manage. My body and mind will never heal to what it once was. Yeah, I've had to work on not being bitter. The hard work of forgiveness is real.

An older, overweight man drove the truck that changed my life. He did not have an agenda to go out and hurt a random person. He just had a job driving a truck and providing for his family.

But alas, there is an "evil villain" in my story who is not the driver. The trucking company allowed the insurance to lapse on their fleet for two days in 2014. Yes, one of them was July 16th, the day of our accident. It is a resolved issue now, and that is all I can say.

The Bible is full of commands to forgive, such as Ephesians 4:32, which says, "Be kind and compassionate to one another, forgiving each other, just as in Christ God forgave you." Those are easy words to say and memorize, but so incredibly hard to live in real life. It is much, much easier said than done.

My time at the hospital in Rancho Los Amigos was shared with the driver. He and his family were there the entire time I was. My mind was still fuzzy and just beginning to heal, but I believe I had only met his wife.

I couldn't find the inner strength to ride my wheelchair upstairs to see him. I never did reach out to him, and I believe he has passed away. I regret not making time to talk through our accident with him. I am grateful Orpha was able to serve his family. She made time to talk with them and even brought them food to share in the waiting rooms.

I would like to have forgiven him face to face. I would like to have said, "I'm sorry," and let him know I did not hold bitterness. I wish

I could have told him face to face how I felt about him and the accident. When I made the decision to forgive, that's how I knew God had really and truly saved me.

I learned a couple of important lessons about forgiveness and letting go of bitterness.

1. **Forgive quickly.** If the Lord or someone is telling you to forgive, get busy and act. Don't wait to "feel like it" because the opportunity may slip through your fingers. We live with less stress and find healing much faster when we choose to forgive. As Ephesians 4:26 says, "In your anger do not sin. Do not let the sun go down while you are still angry."

2. **Admit your wrongs.** We all need forgiveness. Part of losing our pride and forgiving others is also losing our pride and accepting forgiveness when we need it. When you are wrong, say it.

3. **Don't make excuses.** God has not asked us to do an easy thing by forgiving others as Jesus forgives us from the cross. The good news is that we do not have to die or go through physical pain for others to be forgiven. It might feel like we are going to die if we forgive, but thank God, Jesus has already done that for us! We must drop the excuses that keep us from forgiving one another.

Orpha taught me much about forgiveness and how to live it out in our family. She has shown me how to face the cross, get face to face with Jesus, and let go of all the wrongs done to me. Face Jesus with your hurts and pains. Talk honestly with him and then do the hard part; leave your hurts and pains at the foot of the cross.

Forgiveness will change your family. It will teach your children the correct way to handle adversity. Make it a permanent habit.

GOD SHOTS FOR SUCCESS

1. We show our real priorities by how we spend our time and money. How does your family see you use your time? Are you at work? Do you spend more time with hobbies than with your spouse? Take time to reflect and move your time investments to reflect God's call at the crossroads.

2. "Showing up" is more than taking up physical space. Meaningful communication and connection happen when we are fully present with one another. What keeps you from being present? Are those excuses? If Jesus died to be present with us for eternity, what cost would you pay to be present with your family?

3. Addictions rob us of life. Chemical addictions create dependency and change our brain chemistry. I've shared with you how alcohol was destroying me, even though it looked like I "had it all" with a great job and family. Face whatever addiction you have, and ask the Lord to give you freedom. Do the work to break the chains and stay free.

4. Bad things happen to innocent people all the time. Heck, it even happened to me! Our bitterness hurts us and never really touches the other person. Get before the cross and ask Jesus to take away hurts and pains. Take time to pray for your enemies. It is God's path for healing and freedom found in forgiveness.

Chapter 13

SERVICE: GIVING PEOPLE A HAND UP

BY DAVE

"The war is won in the trenches" is a saying we apply not only to warfare but to sports as well. When it comes to American football, it's nearly a religious mantra. Quarterbacks earn the highest salaries, but once you get past them, offensive and defensive linemen also demand high salaries.

Why? Because the war is won in the trenches.

I played lineman in high school and was a walk-on at Oregon State University. The exciting throws of the quarterback, incredible receptions of wide receivers, and spectacular dashes of running backs begin on the line. Offenses are only successful if the talented playmakers can get time and space to move past the other team's front-line defenses.

Linemen do not always make highlight reels, but they set up their teammates for success.

American culture and media give us the idea that we all can and should be superstars. Our culture thrives on big, flashy, loud, game-changing action and the people who make it happen. Sadly, most of us fail to realize that the most valuable contribution you can make is not by being a superstar but by being a great teammate.

WHY SERVE?

Service is living like Jesus. If any person in history had the right to demand others' obedience and personal sacrifice to advance himself, it was Jesus.

But that is just the opposite of how Jesus lived. Paul teaches us that Jesus knew we humans would not understand who He really is. Instead of getting his honor and glory from people, He gave away all the honor and glory that a first-century carpenter and traveling preacher could muster.

When he gave it all away, he served the good of humanity by honoring God and taking away our sin. Paul explains in Philippians 2:1-11.

Therefore, if you have any encouragement from being united with Christ, if any comfort from his love, if any common sharing in the Spirit, if any tenderness and compassion, then make my joy complete by being like-minded, having the same love, being one in spirit and of one mind. Do nothing out of selfish ambition or vain conceit. Rather, in humility value others above yourselves, not looking to your own interests but each of you to the interests of the others.

In your relationships with one another, have the same mindset as Christ Jesus:

> *Who, being in very nature God,*
> > *did not consider equality with God something to be used to his*
> > > *own advantage;*
> *rather, he made himself nothing*
> > *by taking the very nature of a servant,*
> > *being made in human likeness.*
> *And being found in appearance as a man,*
> > *he humbled himself*
> > *by becoming obedient to death—*
> > *even death on a cross!*

> *Therefore, God exalted him to the highest place*
> > *and gave him the name that is above every name,*
> *that at the name of Jesus every knee should bow,*
> > *in heaven and on earth and under the earth,*
> *and every tongue acknowledge that Jesus Christ is Lord,*
> > *to the glory of God the Father.*

American culture has almost turned the word "service" into a curse word. High school kids are told to get "community service hours" so that college entrance boards will accept them. We are conditioned to "serve" to get something back.

Servers build up others. Servers do not look for anything they will receive. Servers know that giving will cost them something, yet they will keep doing it. Servers are not thinking of padding the college or job application. They are not looking to be "understood" in their motives and actions. Servers simply love others the best they can, even when other people might throw it back in their faces.

Jesus made it clear to the disciples that service is a requirement, not an option, for those of us in God's kingdom. In fact, the better we serve (and I mean serving without a thought about getting good things in return), the greater we become. Recall the time when Jesus's disciples were fussing about who was the greatest among them. After listening to the men argue back and forth, Jesus threw them for a loop. He said, "The greatest among you will be your servant. For those who exalt themselves will be humbled, and those who humble themselves will be exalted." (Matthew 23:11-12).

Jesus's statement to the disciples and Paul's reflection on Jesus's life make it clear that service and humility are related. We grow in humility by serving. God wants all of us to embrace humility by serving.

Jesus has already served us with humility and expected us to reject him. Our path to humility, our service, places Jesus's (and others') ideas, plans, and goals above our own.

We serve to become like Jesus. One of the best ways to become like Jesus is to devote some time to a mission trip.

THE VALUE OF MISSION TRIPS

Most of my overseas short-term mission trips were to Central and South America. My first trip was to Belize, and I've also served people in Costa Rica, Ecuador, Honduras, and Mexico. I went as part of construction crews, building schools, churches, and a vocational school in many Central and South American countries.

I made mission trips in those areas mainly to help build schools and churches, pour concrete, erect walls, put up roofs, do electrical work, and whatever else it took to finish a job. We also traveled with doctors, optometrists, and other specialists who ran clinics while we constructed or worked on the buildings.

Serving is the way God's economy grows relationships. Serving is also a learning and connecting opportunity. Every time we choose compassion, mercy, and service, we examine our motives and learn about ourselves. We learn about another person's perspective as a minority, foreigner, opposite gender, different socioeconomic situations, and other experiences we do not have.

These are a few benefits of serving others and taking mission trips. I've experienced this firsthand. Many of my friends who have taken trips have as well.

1. **You will expand your comfort zone.** Humans naturally like routines. We enjoy being around others with common worldviews, habits, and familiar foods. Serving others grows our comfort with others in new situations and expands our experiences.

2. **It is a unique opportunity to hear from the Lord.** Getting away from "normal" can open our minds and hearts to know the Lord differently. We might need new wisdom, insight, or knowledge. Servers often perceive new directions from the Lord because they are in the flow of what God is doing.

3. **You learn what it means to serve without being understood.** John 1 and Philippians 2 tell us that Jesus came to save people who had no clue who he was and the good things he wanted for them. People chased him for performing healing and miracles, then later wanted to kill him. Serving reminds us that we cannot control others and what they might think or say about us. We are free to serve from our best motives.

4. **You will get a glimpse into what it means to live closer to "daily bread."** Most of us in the United States know where our next meal is coming from and how we can pay rent. Economic security was extremely uncommon in Jesus's day and is still uncommon for many today. Serving can grow our appreciation for what we have and for what others lack. It just might change the way we pray like Jesus. "Give us this day our daily bread."

HOW TO GET INVOLVED IN SERVICE

Serving is best done with other people. Jesus sent out the disciples in pairs in Luke 10:1 and Mark 6:7. There is power in prayer and serving with other people. God shows up in special ways; we help bring out the best in our fellow servers, and our motives are more likely to begin and remain pure.

People with a servant's heart always find ways to help and serve others. Many of us need direction and help to grow our "serving muscles." Whether serving is one of our major or minor spiritual gifts, there are many ways for us to join the body of Christ and love the world.

These are a few ways I recommend getting involved in service.

Begin with your Church. I made all of my overseas mission trips through my home church. Our church was a huge supporter of the mission outreach of the Assemblies of God. While our denomination organized the overall mission strategy for thousands of churches and missionaries, it was the mission organization of our local church that helped me get involved with trips, giving, prayer, and more.

Don't overlook local opportunities. People at risk are all around us. Not just the financially poor but the elderly and other "forgotten" people of our culture who need to see the love of Christ in practical terms of service.

Our church got involved with people in our local area. We had a Food Box Ministry in Bakersfield, California. Some of us delivered food boxes to a mobile home park where a lot of elderly people lived. We got to know people through the food deliveries and then found other ways to serve, like fixing fences, repairing wheelchair ramps, and building ramps for those who needed them. Many folks just need to know they aren't forgotten, and that someone loves them.

Poverty is a real problem for people in the United States. The highest poverty rate on record is 22% from the 1950s before President Johnson began the "War on Poverty." The lowest recorded absolute poverty rate is 10.5%, recorded in 2019. The Coronavirus pandemic beginning in 2019 led to an increase in the poverty rate (11.4%) for the first time in nearly forty years. Poverty, like wealth, is not evenly or randomly distributed among Americans.

The U.S. poverty line is pegged at $26,695 for a family of four but affects groups of people in different ways.

Those living in female-headed households with no husband present (24.3%)

Young adults without a high school diploma (23.7%)

Those living in a family whose head is unemployed (26.4%)

Minorities (18.8% for blacks)

Take some time to look around your community. Get some guys together, change the oil, and look over cars for single moms. Look for ways to offer job skills training and rides for those who work, but need some help taking a step forward.

Explore your denomination and other churches. I was blessed with a church that made it easy for me to jump into mission trips. Some churches, especially smaller churches, might not offer the same opportunity to serve. If not, contact your denomination directly and see how you can plug into a trip with other churches.

Go on a mission trip with a local church you know. If your church does not belong to a denomination, look for other churches in your area that take trips. Many people from smaller churches join friends by going on trips organized by their friend's church.

Get involved with mission groups. Hundreds, if not thousands, of independent mission organizations serve native believers, missionaries, and American churches. Google "mission trip" to a place you want to serve, and see how many hits you get!

Set aside money and time. Serving is intentional, and when it is a real priority, we put time and money into our service. Think about vacation and sick days you can spend serving others rather than yourself. Maybe it is just one afternoon—claim it for serving the Lord and volunteering at a soup kitchen. You may only need extra fuel money to get to the soup kitchen or several thousand dollars for an overseas trip. Pray and start setting aside money for serving.

You don't need to wait to use your time and money for serving. Get your priorities set, and the ways to serve will keep jumping out at you!

Ask for a servant's heart. All of us are selfish and prideful. It's a fact that drives us to sin. I know it's not pretty, but let's face it; we all have hard parts of our hearts.

Serving begins with the right motives and attitude, so get it right before the Lord. One of the pitfalls of having plenty of resources, like time and money, is that we don't rely on the Lord. We see our own direction and jump in to "meet a need" without asking God what He thinks about the situation, the person, and our role.

Make prayer the first step in your serving; it will change everything you thought you knew about service.

A HAND *OUT* VERSUS A HAND *UP*

Jesus ends his scolding of the disciples looking to the greatest with these familiar words; "For even the Son of Man did not come to be served, but to serve, and to give his life as a ransom for many." (Mark 10:45)

Looking to be served is a problem of the heart. Some people serve and feel good doing too much for others. What looks like an act of service is really someone getting pleasure by enabling others. On the other hand, plenty of people in the world are happy to take help and never change their lives.

As servants, we need to do our best to help people make changes that move them up in the world without expecting anything in return. Jesus is a perfect example of that. He literally died so we could have eternal life, but He never expected a word of thanks.

A big part of this issue is the attitude of the one receiving help. For instance, my mom was on welfare for a time, but she treated it as a hand-up. She got her finances together and made a new life for herself and my sister. There are so many now treating welfare as a handout. They set up their life to be on welfare forever. We will have more and more kids taking as much as they can from the system. That's not the government's money. It's everyone else's tax money.

In Ephesians 4:28, Paul tells the believers in Ephesus to stop taking and get busy working and living a generous life for others. He says, "Anyone who has been stealing must steal no longer, but must work, doing something useful with their own hands, that they may have something to share with those in need."

Paul also doesn't pull punches with the baby Christians in the baby church of Thessalonica. Evidently, there were some believers who quit working, thinking Jesus would come back very soon. They thought there was no point in working since they would go to heaven soon. Paul had a different point of view.

He says, "For even when we were with you, we gave you this rule; 'The one who is unwilling to work shall not eat.' We hear that some among you are idle and disruptive. They are not busy; they are busybodies. Such people we command and urge in the Lord Jesus Christ to settle down and earn the food they eat." (2 Thessalonians 3:10-12)

When President Franklin Roosevelt originally started the WPA (Works Progress Administration), Social Security, and other aspects of safety net programs, the idea was to help people get on their feet and get back in the workforce. Working-aged people were expected to rejoin the workforce and get back to generating income. Older people were given enough income to survive.

But now, government programs are viewed too much as a handout instead of a hand-up. Most people want to be a contributing member of society. Most people want to make their own money and create their own place in the world with their own wealth.

A problem with a lot of young folks is that they have not been taught to make their own way in life. They have no sense of pride in earning money themselves or developing wealth themselves. Too many people want others to give it to them.

A big attitude has developed against people who have jobs and have made money. The excuse for not doing the same is, "Hey, those people are greedy. That's why they have all the money." Well, that might or might not be true. But when they create wealth by investing in companies, they are creating jobs. Those jobs create an avenue for others to create their own wealth. I think this idea of working and helping others to work is missed by a lot of people in our culture.

Many parents have missed the mark on raising their kids the right way. When you raise a godly child, they will want to be a contributor. Living by serving and giving generously is part of what it means to be a disciple of Jesus. Kids grow up to be givers and not takers. They will look at help as a hand-up and not a handout.

HOW TO GET STARTED

Ultimately, it all comes down to actually doing something. It's one thing to talk about serving, but quite another to push pause on all the chatter and begin taking action.

Serving can start either by doing or thinking. Getting our thinking right will move us toward doing the right things. Doing the right thing can help us think the right way. I cannot emphasize this enough; pray about a place where you need to start and the type of ways you learn. Don't think too much. Just jump in and start serving! I want to offer you four suggestions.

1. **Be ready to serve and not be served.** I remember one guy on a trip who was a senior welder. He was highly regarded by the other welders but was so arrogant. He was used to being a union boss and only doing his portion of the work. Unfortunately, he carried his union boss style to the mission field, and he would say, "Hey, could you pick those things up and carry them for me?" The rest of us would say, "No, you can carry your own things."

   He expected someone else to carry his stuff everywhere. We had to remind him this was not a union site and that he volunteered, just like everyone else, to work on this trip. It was an education for everyone.

   I have to thank God this guy had a chance to learn about service. Get your mind ready to serve. If it is not ready, just jump in and do something—God will iron out your rough edges.

2. **Talk to your spouse about money and time.** Serving starts by making others a priority with your time and money. Don't just decide this on your own. American culture makes it easy for one spouse to get into serving. Men's groups, women's groups, and all kinds of other groups are easy to be a part of and find people to serve with. Don't leave your spouse out of this journey! Talk about the ways God is calling both of you to prioritize time and money for serving.

3. **Talk with your pastor.** Your pastor has a network of people and ideas for serving. Ask your pastor for a few minutes to talk about missions and other serving passions and ideas you have. Pastors will know what is happening inside and outside the church and guide you toward the center of God's calling in your life. You are not alone on this journey.

4. **Go with the passions God has given you.** God gives different gifts to all his children. We are not the same, but parts of a

body. So don't start by serving in an area where you have no interest, talent, or ideas. Start with what you know, and enjoy the way God has made you to serve. Look for mission trips that will use your gifts.

TWO IMPORTANT LESSONS

I know this has been a challenging chapter. Our natural human tendency is to want other people to serve us instead of serving others. I appreciate you hanging in there with me, as I've offered thoughts sure to make you a bit uncomfortable at times. I close this chapter by offering two key lessons I've learned from those I have served over the years.

Those lessons are *joy* and *gratitude*. I have seen a lady with a big smile on her face sweeping a dirt floor in a little shanty, lean-to-type house made from pallets. Inside, her husband watched a tiny TV in the corner. Their kids were out front playing a game with a little tattered ball and some sort of stick. She swept her dirt floor, enjoying the love of her family and the love of the Lord.

Here in America, we have a huge gratitude problem. We have stores full of goods, even with high inflation. Even with supply chain problems during a pandemic, we have food. Everything is so readily available. If you go to a supermarket in Venezuela, Cuba, and other countries, it will be empty. People live without things and enjoy the things they have. There is a lot we can learn from that.

When I think about that woman who was sweeping, her focus was not on things but on people. I believe this comes only from a relationship with the Lord through knowing our heavenly father and accepting his love through Jesus.

True joy and gratitude are different from the happiness the world offers. The world tells us, "When you have _____, then you will be happy." They try to fill in the blank with cars, sex, money, power, time, and a thousand other things. Until we choose to fill the blank in our life with Jesus, we will never find the joy we can have through knowing Him and serving the people He died for.

GOD SHOTS FOR SUCCESS

1. When you read Paul's words in Philippians chapter 2 about serving, what is your response? Does the difficulty and challenge of serving make you want to be more like Jesus? Does it draw you to Him?

2. In this chapter, I have emphasized mission trips as an important way to serve Jesus and others. Have you ever been on a mission trip? If so, what was your experience? If you haven't yet been on one, think about a time frame when you could realistically participate in one. It will change your life, I promise!

3. As you consider making money and building a career, do you feel you should make your own way in the world and be a giver instead of a taker? That may sound like a simple question, but take a moment to really think about it. Are you willing to work hard, learn, and grow so you can be a big contributor to society?

4. Do you have a gratitude practice? How do you show God and others you are thankful for what you have?

Chapter 14

FINANCES: TRUSTING GOD WITH YOUR TREASURE

BY DAVE

I n the last chapter, we discussed the difference between a handout and a hand-*up*. The reality is that sometimes *you* are the person who needs a hand up.

After my accident, I lost my job. We were flat broke and lost our house. Some of that was my fault. We had a ton of medical bills, no relief from the trucking company that didn't have insurance on its rig, and limited income. I was still technically employed by the company and could not use my 401(k). All the money I had in savings was quickly drained.

But suddenly, when we really needed help, checks started to show up in the mail. One week, checks totaling $4,000 came in. Another week, $5,000, then $3,000 showed up.

I had no idea where it all came from. I still have no idea why it showed up or whose accounts it came from. So many things like that happened over the last eight years; it taught me an important lesson. Without a doubt, God's blessing is tied to how we follow Jesus. We had been honest and loyal, willing to give the shirts off our backs, and people were willing to help us.

God used many people to give us the hand-*up* we desperately needed.

It's nothing short of a miracle that we've been blessed so much in the last eight years. I was blessed when I was working; I thought because I earned good money and had a nice house. But I feel more blessed now than when I had all those things. That's the honest truth.

WHERE ARE YOUR PRIORITIES?

It can be tough to talk about finances because people are very private about it. Fair enough. I don't have any interest in prying into your personal life. However, I do want to ask you one simple question.

Where are your priorities?

I believe the answer to that question is fairly simple. You don't have to guess where your priorities lie. You can find them where you spend your time and money.

People can get caught in the trap of thinking they will give time and money when they can afford it. They set up milestones of success, which become millstones in their relationship with God.

The rich young man had this problem. In Mark 10:17-31, Jesus confronts a young man who "has it all together." He is young. He is rich. He is a good man. He asks Jesus what else is needed to enter the Kingdom of heaven. From the way he approaches Jesus, and the way

Jesus responds to him, the young man is probably very earnest. He felt like he had all the "milestones" in life figured out and was asking Jesus what it takes to get more out of this life and the next.

But Jesus told him to sell everything he had, give it to the poor, and follow Him. When the rich young man turned away from Jesus, those milestones became millstones that kept him from following Jesus and getting the life he wanted.

God is not waiting for you to make him the priority of your life tomorrow. He wants you to live for him today. The widow in Mark 12:41-44 gave everything she had in the temple in a quiet, small way. She gave more than the loud, rich man who trumpeted his way into the temple announcing the big gift he was leaving. His milestone gift became a millstone that day.

God will pay you back more than you could ever give. It's hard for a lot of people to believe you can't out-give God. People hear that and think, *Yeah, whatever.* God's giving into my life has been nothing short of a blessing.

ABG: ALWAYS BE GENEROUS

Generosity is a habit and mindset that you can practice all the time. When you describe someone as "generous with their time," that person does not wait for a special occasion or make it difficult to share their thoughts and expertise.

Generous giving is the same way. You don't need to wait for a special occasion to share.

Jesus drove his disciples crazy with his generosity! They tried to shoo away children and their parents because Jesus was busy. But Jesus said, "Let the children come to me." He was on the way to see the daughter of an important synagogue leader named Jarius, yet stopped in the middle of a rush to speak with a woman who had been bleeding for twelve years. Jesus taught all day and talked for so long it was too late for the crowd of 5,000 men, plus all the women and children, to find food.

Jesus told the disciples to fix the problem! And when they couldn't, He blessed two fish and five loaves of bread. Then the disciples fed all the men, women, and children. Generosity is not always convenient. It might make people uncomfortable. That's okay. It's just living like Jesus.

I like to give money away when I'm in a restaurant. Maybe it's a 150% tip or something like that. I like to bless people where I can. Maybe it's a single mom serving the coffee during the breakfast rush. I've been in there enough times to know that person has it rough. With a little bit of help, she can make her car payment this month. That little extra can help her do more for her family.

I'm looking for ways to share with people and be generous. This is not necessarily from my God Account, which is my planned giving, but the extra money I carry with me to share.

THE GOD ACCOUNT

I cannot earn income now. I live on a fixed income fueled partly by my 401(k). My disability keeps me home. The trucking company kept us from being as financially whole as we had planned to be in retirement. In fact, it's not even close (can you feel my eyes roll here?). But I knew I needed to keep giving, and I wanted to give as much to the Lord as I could, so I made my God Account.

My God Account is money I've set aside for planned giving in the Kingdom of God. When I gained access to my 401(k), I did what I've always done. I set 10% of my portfolio aside for God. Nothing revolutionary, but it makes a big difference in the way I give.

Just like I did with my other earned income, I took my retirement money and made 10% of it a tithe. My God Account is 10% of my total retirement, and I use earnings for planned giving, which matches my fixed income.

You don't need a traumatic brain injury like I have in order to be disciplined with money, especially giving. My giving money is set aside. I cannot just take that money and put it into a church, a ministry, or missionary all at one time. The God Account is the tool enabling me to spend and grow Kingdom money over my lifetime. I am free to give as I feel led and know I have money to give down the road when I'm called to give.

Here's one way to do it; take whatever amount you have in retirement accounts, settlements, bonds, or whatever. Earmark 10% of that and make a God Account. There are two parts to stewarding what God has given to you. First, the money can grow and earn interest on itself under your management and care. Second, you can spend the money to advance God's Kingdom.

The best part of the God Account is the giving! Having something to give is a blessing, and growing assets for the Lord is a special stewardship blessing, too. But giving where the Lord is leading us to be a part of his Kingdom is where the rubber hits the road. Money and time are part of detaching from the world and staying attached to Jesus.

By setting aside 10% of my 401(k) into my God Account, I know what I have to spend for tithing. So, I do it! I give to my church, mission trips, special offerings, and wherever my heart and mind desire.

A young lady at our church befriended Orpha and me. She needed $1,000 for a summer mission trip. I was able to give it to her because the money was in the God Account. Another gentleman we know has a daughter serving as a missionary in India. She and her husband were asking for $1,000, but I knew they needed more. I looked in the God Account, prayed, and sent them $5,000.

These are just two people I knew and wanted to support. I believe in them and their ministries. Because of the God Account, they get to live out God's calling on their lives.

This has been an adjustment for me. I used to be able to spend money on things like car repairs and giving to missionaries without much thought. Sure, things might be tight for a week or two, but there was always new money flowing in and a growing 401(k). Now, I can't take spending for granted. Orpha reminds me all the time to watch my spending because we are now on a fixed income. The God Account helps both of us to manage our giving and our expectations on a fixed income.

Partnering with God, using your time and money to achieve His desires, is a lifelong calling for disciples of Jesus.

TITHING & GIVING

You don't suddenly become a generous giver with a God Account when you retire. Giving our time and money are spiritual muscles we build by using them often. Just like the simple habit of taking a daily walk can lead to a lifetime of physical health, the simple habit of tithing and giving leads to a lifetime of spiritual health.

I know tithing sounds "old-fashioned," but it's still important. The author of Hebrews pointed out how he tithed before Moses even had the law. That means he gave 10% of the spoils of war to the high priest and King Melchizedek. Tithing in the Old Testament, and in Jesus's day, was a declaration that everything a person has, all 100%, comes from God.

Be sure to give your top 10% to the Lord. Donations you make to God's Kingdom above tithing are called gifts in the Bible. Be generous with your tithing and giving.

Paul gives us clear instructions in 2 Corinthians 9:6-8. He says:

Remember this: Whoever sows sparingly will also reap sparingly, and whoever sows generously will also reap generously. Each of you should give what you have decided in your heart to give, not reluctantly or under compulsion, for God loves a cheerful giver. And God is able to bless you abundantly, so that in all things at all times, having all that you need, you will abound in every good work.

The New Testament standard for giving is different than the Old Testament. Our standard is not the law but the generous love of God given to us through the life, death, and resurrection of Jesus. So, get generous and get cheerful! We are part of bringing God's hopes and dreams into this world.

Why wait until retirement to begin stewarding money for the Lord? You can start a God Account and let it grow! Maybe you start small with deposits in a savings or money market account where you can access it easily when needed. Perhaps you have additional income you can grow in an investment account. There is no need to wait when planning your generosity.

When you have money set aside, you can spend from the account to do whatever you want for God. If you are led to help someone fix a handicap ramp or a house—maybe even to go somewhere to do God's work where you cannot go—you can pull it from that account.

Make a plan to cheerfully give and get ready to see God bless you with relationships and a closer walk with Him as you get directly involved in His work here on earth.

GOD IS FAITHFUL!

The Bible is full of stories of God being faithful to His children. No doubt, you have heard missionaries tell stories of God being faithful. Maybe you have witnessed God's faithfulness to a friend or someone in your church.

Why do we wonder if God will be faithful to us? Maybe it is because we want to be self-sufficient and in control. Maybe we are more concerned about what we can do for God rather than living by faith, totally dependent on God.

Consider Matthew 19:23-25, which says:

Then Jesus said to his disciples, "Truly I tell you, it is hard for someone who is rich to enter the kingdom of heaven. Again I tell you, it is easier for a camel to go through the eye of a needle than for someone who is rich to enter the kingdom of God." When the disciples heard this, they were greatly astonished and asked, "Who then can be saved?"

Maybe we think too much like the disciples. Jesus makes this statement when the rich young man turns away from Jesus and back to his millstone of wealth. The disciples are thinking, *Hey, if a young guy with all the money and time in the world can't figure out how to get into heaven, what hope is there for any of the rest of us?*

Indeed, the Kingdom of God is upside down. It's for those who desperately throw themselves with all their identity, wealth, dignity, love, dreams, hopes, and fears into the hands of a God they cannot see. God is faithful to those who trust him with everything.

I mention this because I've seen the rich, deep river of God's faithfulness when my family and I needed Him most. It is not a blessing just for us. God is ready to be faithful to you.

Orpha faced a tough time when I was in a coma, and we were all living in the hospital. She was worried about our insurance coming to an end. I was in a coma, and the hospital doctors and staff said all that was left was to take me to a nursing home. The insurance company said they were finished paying for hospital treatment because I was not going to get better. They didn't say it, but they meant I was just going to transfer to the nursing home and die.

My boss, Dave, heard about all this and asked the hospital staff, "Where's the best place for Dave Blanchat?"

They replied, "Well, right here."

"All right," Dave said, "Then he stays. Whatever insurance does not pay, we will pay."

What a God Shot! Dave and the company's support immediately lifted the financial burden from Orpha. Before the accident, I made enough money for all of us and took care of the bills. The accident turned Orpha's life upside-down; the last thing she needed to worry about was money.

God proved faithful after the hospital stay. I was in my first rehabilitation assignment near Ranch Los Amigos, and Orpha had to say in a hotel. She stayed for my rehab during days forty-one through eighty. When she went to check out, the hotel bill had been covered.

We have no idea who covered the hotel bill. I know it wasn't my family. They don't have that kind of money, let alone faith in God. So, it had to be something greater. Something more was going on. Maybe it was my company. Maybe it was someone else. I'm not sure, but her hotel bill was covered.

My eyes are open to the possibility that God works. I keep seeing God Shots in other people's lives. My brother-in-law was on the verge of losing his job. I don't know how many months he was out of work before they called him back, but he didn't lose his job. There are smaller God Shots, such as people needing to go on mission trips, not having the money, then the money coming from donations.

These are life-changing events made possible through a faithful God. I have no idea why these things happen to me, my brother-in-law, or others. The only explanation is that God makes a way where there is no way.

DON'T BE THE ONE WHO MISSES EVERYTHING

In the classic 1980s movie *Ferris Bueller's Day Off*, the main character, Ferris (played by Matthew Broderick), says, "Life moves pretty fast. If you don't stop and look around once in a while, you could miss it." He said that in the context of missing a day of high school, but the truth applies to life in general.

We need to take time to pay attention to the life happening around us. If we don't, we're in danger of missing everything.

Paul reminded us in 2 Corinthians that God loves a cheerful giver. The opposite of being cheerful is selfishness, and we have too many selfish people in the world. Selfish people look out for themselves and miss all the life going on around them.

Think about what it means to be selfish—making every decision for yourself. Selfish people cannot serve. Selfish people cannot be grateful. Selfish people cannot be cheerful. Selfish people do not have room in their lives for such things. They are too busy with their own plans, pains, and ideas. One of the biggest problems in the world is that we have far too many selfish people.

Generous people are, by definition, looking for the opposite. They want and have pure motives for helping, serving, and giving. They step away from the foolishness of the flesh and live in the fullness of how God made humans.

The Lord intends for us to serve and love one another with generous spirits. He wants us to become people who depend on Him for everything, who know He is the source of everything, who are grateful for the good things He gives them, and who see His faithful generosity. It's those people who can give cheerfully. They are the people who are truly living.

This cheerful giver thing does not happen overnight and is not just a feeling of being happy. No, this is an attitude of serving and enjoying being part of God's Kingdom and bringing God's love to the world.

People with the attitude of gratitude become cheerful givers. They are the ones who look for ways to say, "Thank you, Lord" more than, "Why me, Lord?" Grateful people are thankful for each day of life and the next moments of taking a breath. Cheerful people are grateful for their spouses, kids, and everyone they know. That's why they are so pleasant to live with!

I went through a season, letting pain and the losses from the accident rob me of being grateful. I was a jerk and thought I had a right to be a jerk. I was feeling broken. But now, I am grateful to be alive. I'm grateful for one more breath. I'm grateful to share one more moment with my kids. I'm grateful for one more moment with my wife, a chance to see the sky, and one more glimpse of the clouds. I'm grateful for everything. Everything!

Ungrateful people are selfish and conceited. They miss so much of life. They miss everything that is beautiful in this world.

If you are not grateful, you miss everything.

PRACTICAL STEPS TO BEING GENEROUS

All the qualities we discussed—generosity, stewardship, and cheerfulness—are cultivated by habits. The process of making a habit can be fast or slow, but it is always intentional. We may have "accidental" habits we learned as kids and carry into adulthood. We might have thought and money habits we inherited, but we have chosen to keep them.

I want you to experience a financial life in the center of God's faithfulness, bombarded with God Shots. While you don't need to invest thousands of dollars, you can invest your life in actions that shape your heart, soul, and mind toward the Lord.

Also, remember that generosity is not just an attitude we have with money. Generosity is not being selfish with any part of our lives. Here are a few practical ideas:

1. **Stop at yellow lights and pick the long check-out lane**. "Patience is a virtue" is not in the Bible, but patience is a fruit of the spirit. Make yourself be patient by choosing to slow

down and take your time. Patience is not just about accepting the time you have to wait. It is also being at peace during the waiting. Don't smash the gas pedal, trying to make the light before it turns red. Instead, slow down, and wait.

2. **Don't do distracting things while you drive.** I can't tell you how many people I've seen doing crazy things on the road in my twenty years of driving—ladies putting on their makeup and filing their nails, and guys shaving while driving, stopped at a light, at a stop sign, or waiting for a pedestrian. You may think, *It will never happen to me* until it does.

3. **Brighten the day of a clerk**. For example, when you visit a gas station, you can make someone's day by just saying, "Hello, how are you?" and smiling. It really is as simple as that. You don't need a coach or someone to teach you how to be kind and show gratitude. Simple acts of kindness are a good place to start. The more successful and further you get in life, the more important these acts of kindness are to keep us rooted in others.

4. **Don't buy the $5 latte at Starbucks**. Don't squander money on useless things. Choose to stay at home and eat out less. You will save money and have more time to cook at home and hang out with your wife and kids.

5. **Start with an attitude of being grateful for this life**. "I'll be grateful." Those can be hard words to say when we have trouble in our past, but it is a place for all of us to start. Pain and sin can turn us inward, making us selfish and conceited. Start by saying, "I'm grateful for life." It becomes easy to do things like tip, encourage others, and keep your opinion to yourself.

6. **Look for what is right in the world.** Humans can always find things that are wrong with the world. The Prince of the World is always out and about messing with governments, international

politics, and even with people we love. But, you know, it's a lot harder to say, "This is what is right with the world. This is what's right with what's going on in life." When you can see what is good, pure, and right, you can solve a lot of problems.

If you decide those things in your heart and truly take God at His word, the rest will come. Start with little things and build, step by step, toward the bigger ways to serve in life. Don't wait for big God Shots. In fact, don't expect anything from the Lord. Just serve and love without thinking of yourself. Let God lead you where he wants you to go.

GOD SHOTS FOR SUCCESS

1. You've heard many stories in this chapter (and book) about God Shots—how God miraculously provided for us in times of need. What are some ways God has done the same for you? Can you think of any God Shots in your life involving money or finances?

2. After reading my thoughts on starting a God Account, how might you put that into practice? What kind of blessings could God bring into your life if you do it?

3. Many people feel funny talking about money. In our American culture, it is almost taboo to challenge people's attitudes toward money. Do you feel challenged or a little uncomfortable by this chapter? Why or why not? Is it good to be uncomfortable at times?

4. Look over the Practical Steps to Being Generous I listed above. Which of those could you put into practice over the next few days? Generosity doesn't need to be overly complicated. Just give it a shot, and you will be amazed at the wonderful things that begin to happen!

Chapter 15

CREATION: ENJOYING THE GREAT OUTDOORS

BY DAVE

I love God's creation. One of the things I have missed most since my accident is the freedom to explore and play in God's masterpiece. God made the earth for us to enjoy without buildings, pavement, concrete highways, or anything else on it. My soul soars, and I enjoy creation just as God designed it.

I'm the guy who enjoys hiking off-trail and striking a virgin path in the wilderness with my buddies. I like fishing where I cannot see anyone else on the water. Fishing is better in a spot I think no one has ever been to.

What would it be like to fill your lungs with oxygen untouched by humans? Did Adam and Eve open their eyes in wonder at the colors, sounds, and smells that rushed into their brains? What kind of words or sounds passed through their minds and from their lips when they saw their hands for the first time?

King David wrote in Psalms 19:1-2,

The heavens declare the glory of God;
the skies proclaim the work of his hands.
Day after day they pour forth speech;
night after night they reveal knowledge.

Those words perfectly express how I feel when I spend time in God's majestic creation.

I can't help but feel an overwhelming sense of wonder and mystery in a universe of swirling galaxies, roving black holes, and innumerable stars and planets of all shapes and sizes.

Nowhere is the universe more amazing, wonderful, and chaotic than here on planet earth, where God stirred life from nothing. Earth is where Almighty God chose to make and share life with humans in an environment made to bring us goodness.

Hiking is one of the many ways I love to get out of civilization and into God's creation. One of my favorite hikes was over Ritter Pass with a couple of buddies of mine from work. Most of the hike was off-trail on a river path reaching an altitude of almost 12,000 feet. We hiked from the west side of the Sierra Mountains, over Ritter Pass at the Minarets, to the east side of the Sierra Mountains, with glacier lakes all around us at elevation on the west side.

God's work at Ritter Pass swept me into this masterpiece of creation as He intended us to see it—a beautiful, untouched, unspoiled place. As we hiked, we heard the shale shifting under our feet. It was kind of ominous, yet at the same time, so much fun! We took a step, and the rocks where our feet landed were still, but we'd hear the shale beneath them moving.

WAITING FOR HEALING

One of the most fascinating parts of my journey over the last several years is seeing how my brokenness parallels the brokenness of creation. But it's not just me—we are all broken in probably more ways than we can count. My body is broken, and so is my spirit. Yours is, too. We are all incomplete and are all waiting for the day when we will be healed and restored in heavenly perfection.

I relate to what Paul wrote in Romans 8:18-25 about creation:

I consider that our present sufferings are not worth comparing with the glory that will be revealed in us. For the creation waits in eager expectation for the children of God to be revealed. For the creation was subjected to frustration, not by its own choice, but by the will of the one who subjected it, in hope that the creation itself will be liberated from its bondage to decay and brought into the freedom and glory of the children of God.

We know that the whole creation has been groaning as in the pains of childbirth right up to the present time. Not only so, but we ourselves, who have the first fruits of the Spirit, groan inwardly as we wait eagerly for our adoption to sonship, the redemption of our bodies. For in this hope we were saved. But hope that is seen is no hope at all. Who hopes for what they already have? But if we hope for what we do not yet have, we wait for it patiently.

These verses give me hope that our present sufferings are only temporary. And it's a good thing, too, because healing has been rough. I can no longer go for hikes, especially in a place like Ritter Pass. I feel close to God when I'm outside and in creation. I don't just miss golf, hiking, fishing, diving, and running. I miss meeting God and sharing His presence in unspoiled and remote parts of creation with friends and family.

Luckily, my injuries do not keep me from fly fishing, although it's much harder now. I started fly fishing in Oregon as a young adult but never really became a fly fisherman until I met my AA sponsor, John. He got me hooked on it, and I bought rods, reels, flies, a vest, a net, and all the other equipment.

After the accident, I tried fly fishing with John and others at the Broken Neck Trout Campout in California. I really struggled. Two of the biggest obstacles were getting in and out of my float tube because of my foot and stiff body, and also tying knots with double vision. I had to laugh at myself. When I finally got into my float tube, my fused ankle made me spin in circles!

Even though I've been through a lot of pain and frustration, I can laugh at these crazy situations because God will ultimately restore everything, including you and me. It's laughable how we try to control every element of our lives. God is the One who is in control, not you and me.

As the Scripture above says, creation is groaning for restoration. We are waiting for Jesus to return and make a new heaven and new earth. I'm looking forward to that day too. We have lost the wholeness and perfection of the Garden of Eden, but we will return to it one day.

MY LOVE LANGUAGE WITH GOD

Every person has a natural pathway for connecting with God. Contemplatives love prayer. Activists get into causes. Servants help people. Teachers study and speak. Musicians enjoy songs, hymns, and praise music.

I'm a naturalist. My natural connection to God is in the outdoors. I feel closer to God and more at peace with myself when I'm fishing where there is no one in sight. When I've hunted where others have not tracked down a deer or pitched my tent in forgotten places of the world, I am close to God.

I miss diving at night. When a nature lover like me gets to the ocean floor and shuts off the light, surrounded by nothing by watery darkness, it is an otherworldly experience. Then when you throw the light switch back on and see crabs scurrying over rocks, kelp, coral, and each other, you feel the rush of being alive. You get to experience something few people ever see. It's almost overwhelming.

One of the most amazing experiences you will ever have is taking a night dive beside the kelp forests growing from the ocean floor to the surface surrounding the Catalina Islands. When you shake the kelp, bio-luminescent organisms come floating off in showers of brilliant light. What a stunning sight. This is God's garden, right there for us to enjoy if we know where to look and when to turn off the lights.

I wish I could golf as I used to, but that is more or less out of the question. I was never a scratch golfer, but I had a nine handicap and a membership at the local country club through my job. Now, even the thought of golfing hurts. Among other things, my shoulders don't enjoy being twisted and contorted during a golf swing. If I do play golf, it's with friends from AA and strictly for fun.

I prided myself on being independent, then had the accident. Maybe God is allowing me to feel true dependence as a part of creation. I am learning to depend on my wife, nurses, caregivers, therapists, and Him.

I get a little melancholy as I sift through these memories because being out and about with God is one of the biggest things I miss. I miss the spiritual connection. I miss being able to talk to God as I walk, sit on a rock, or bask in the sun. To me, feeling the wind ruffling my hair and whistling past my ears is like listening to God's voice.

I miss it so much. I know He created the earth for us to enjoy with Him, to commune with Him on a personal level. There is no deeper spiritual satisfaction than walking with the Lord through the woods, over the rocks, or up a mountain.

I remember hiking Mount Whitney before I got saved. It was a blast. I had a wicked headache at the peak of a 14,000-foot-tall mountain! But I would have enjoyed it much more if I had known and understood God's role in everything in the universe. The hike, the peak, and even the headache would have been a much different experience if I had known Jesus as my Creator and Savior.

At the time of this writing, it has been eight years since my accident. These days, I don't meet God in remote mountain passes, but I see Him in creation. I praise the Lord for my yard, the river running close to my house, the surrounding mountains, the trees, and even the birds chirping and singing around me. Thank you, God, for your wonderful creation.

I'm baffled by those who believe in the complete randomness of evolution. It's like believing that rocks can fall down a mountain and land at the bottom arranged as intricately as a watch with all its minuscule gears, springs, and sprockets.

Evolution does exist on a micro scale. Everything adapts or evolves to fit its environment. Organisms change in order to stay alive over the long term. But the sheer awesomeness of the universe, from the intergalactic pulses of stars down to the smallest bits of quarks, cannot be adequately explained by a *big bang*.

Or maybe it can. God spoke, and bang, the universe was born! I trust in the truth of the Bible even if we, as humans, may not understand how everything works. Maybe one day in heaven, God will explain it all to us.

BUILDING YOUR RELATIONSHIPS THROUGH THE OUTDOORS

Spending time outdoors over the years made my relationships stronger, deeper, and full of shared experiences. I went hiking and shooting with friends. I enjoyed hikes with Paige, my daughter. Orpha and I spent time together scuba diving. When I think about meeting God in the outdoors, I also think about the great people with whom I have gotten to share my life. Sharing God's creation made unique connections with my friends and family I will cherish for the rest of my life.

The week before my accident is a blur. I remember the shoot final for my precision rife class, and that's about it. My friends Dave, Conan, and I were dropped off at 1:00 or 2:00 a.m. and had to make it to the predefined shoot spot before sunrise, undetected, and be ready to take our shots to several hundred meters at sunrise. The entire time, guys were out looking for us. We did it!

I spent a lot of time with these guys and others at work I hiked with sometimes. It made our relationships grow to new levels. Whether it was crunching shale on the trail or a 3:00 a.m. sniper test, these shared experiences bonded us together. I am grateful for this brotherly love.

By the way, I'm getting back into long-range shooting at 1,000 to 2,000+ yards. Praise the Lord!

Orpha and I went on our second honeymoon to a Bonaire, a diver's island in the ABC islands. It was a special time for us to experience diving together. To be honest, it was not so much for Orpha's enjoyment but for us to make memories and share time together. My wife is an amazing woman. She was scared to death of the water before taking lessons, but she took up diving because I dove and loved it. Her love for me was greater than her fear of water. Diving together built up our marriage on a very personal level.

My daughter and I had such a good time hiking the Painted Cave in central California. Once, we hiked through an area that had a recent hatch of earwigs. They were huge, and the swarm was massive. There is nothing quite like a mass of flying insects landing on you and pinching away!

Paige just sucked it up and kept on walking through the earwigs. I really enjoyed trips out with my daughter. We'd be heading home from a campsite, and I'd shout, "Truck check!" Paige would look in the bed and make sure everything was riding safe and secure. I look back on that as an awesome experience because we did it together.

One time, I was winter hiking with a group, and we got to an area where there were millions of ladybugs in a wooded area. They covered sticks, snow, tree stumps, branches, and every bare place in the winter woods. Unfortunately for us, it was getting late, and we needed to make camp with the ladybugs. So, we laid out our tents, got out our sleeping bags, and it was soon time to go to bed.

The ladybugs got into the tents, looking for a place to get warm for the night. Unfortunately, that place was our sleeping bags! We had to shake them out and zip the bag up so tight that it was uncomfortable. Those ladybugs were determined!

We formed bonds of brotherly love because of the hike and the ladybugs. We were never in danger and were safe from bears, mountain lions, and other dangers of creation. We were free to just have fun and make memories together in the presence of God in creation.

I think that is what God intended—people being outdoors together, getting unguarded and real with one another.

Orpha and I still get out in nature in our RV. We took our time finding a motor home that did not have a "doghouse" in the center between the passenger and driver. My right foot's kind of stuck at ninety degrees, and getting around that doghouse was too much.

Orpha had her concerns, but she proved once again how strong and capable she is. She found a trainer in Boise willing to give us some classes. He set up cones for us to slalom through, going forward and backward. He also set up a mock loading dock so we could practice backing up the RV. Orpha nailed it every time! She parallel-parked it like a boss. She backed it up into the loading dock like a boss. She slalomed like a boss, both forward and backward! The guy said she could go from that class and get her commercial driver's license for a big rig.

We may have traded diving for driving, but God keeps giving us the grace to share time together in nature.

WHAT IF YOU'RE NOT AN "OUTDOORS" PERSON?

You may not connect with God in nature as I do, but it is still a good place to worship and meet God with your family. Who knows, one of them may share my love language and find a special sense of God's presence in the great outdoors. The best part of being outdoors is having intentional time together and making memories. Even if something goes wrong—for example, dealing with millions of ladybugs—you can turn it into a funny family story for years to come.

You don't have to buy a lot of special equipment or carve out days and weeks to enjoy the outdoors with your family. Get creative and look at what you can do. Here are a few ideas.

Take your kids to the park and play! Go somewhere outdoors where you feel free. Spend an hour playing and walking around. Instead of shooting hoops in the gym or tossing a baseball on a field, just take them to a park setting. It feels more in tune with nature.

Go concrete camping. If you're averse to roughing it outdoors without electricity and water, go concrete camping. This refers to a campground made by the forest service, state, or city. There will be running water, pit toilets, shower houses, and maybe even full-fledged bathrooms. Grab a tent and try it out!

Get curious. As you drive down the road and something looks cool, pull the car over and investigate with your kids. Imagine the scenarios. "Hey, kids, what kinds of trees are these? Let's go check it out!" "Oh, where does this stream go? Let's look!" Curiosity can take you places you would otherwise never discover.

Visit a point of interest. Head to a state or federal park without much of an agenda. Plan to look at a waterfall, a stream, a river, or a hiking trail. Work your way up to being comfortable with fishing, then take your kids out fishing and camping in a new place.

Start in your backyard. Start with what is simple and familiar, which means your backyard. Get a tent and have your family camp with you in the backyard. If you don't have a backyard, borrow one from a friend for a night or two. Maybe their family will join you!

Don't let fear of the unknown keep you from God's creation. Trust that God wants you in his playground. Find places outside where you are more comfortable. It can be as simple as taking your kids to the park. You will build confidence with each experience as you try new things. Being outdoors gives you an opportunity to intentionally be with your family.

One final tip; build a fire if you can. Good memories happen around fires!

HOW TO GET STARTED ON A SMALL BUDGET

As you read this chapter, you may be thinking, *Dave, all of this sounds wonderful, but I have no budget for camping, fishing trips, diving, or any other activities.* That's okay. The important thing is not necessarily the "bigness" of the activity. It's far more important that you simply do *something*. Plus, many great memories can be made doing things that don't cost a dime or cost very little.

A great place to start is by doing a campout in the living room. Plan on eating outside in your backyard or at a nearby park. Roast some hot dogs and marshmallows, then head back to the house.

No sleeping bags? No problem! Make up some beds in the living room and "camp" together in one place. No extra money is required to make memories and spend time together.

Your next step could be adding air mattresses for your next living room campout. Add some headlamps for your kids and tell stories outside after dark. Then come back home and keep the lights off. Find a cheap tent at a garage sale or on clearance, and you are ready to do a backyard campout or go concrete camping.

Being outside, together with your friends and family, is not about having a lot of special equipment. It is all about making time to be with each other. Look for fishing, hiking, and camping equipment sales during the fall and winter so you can score some great deals. Don't worry about buying things all at once. Start picking things up over the next few months, and soon you'll be enjoying God's playground!

Take time to catch a fish with your son or daughter. Identify animals and their tracks when you're out hiking. Point out trees, bushes, and wildflowers in the woods. These are all ways to build precious memories for you and your kids.

You have one shot at making the most of the time you have been given. Once time is gone, it doesn't come back around again.

GOD SHOTS FOR SUCCESS

1. What is your "love language" with God? How does it interact with creation and give you a bigger picture of who God is? In order to expand your faith, try combining prayer with sitting outside. Use a Psalm or the Lord's Prayer to praise God while sitting in His creation.

2. Being in nature is a potential act of worship. We can meet God, think about our place in the universe, and see His creative abundance. Take a walk and notice nature. What is going well? What needs to be restored? How are you helping the restoration of the planet?

3. How do you need to develop a theology of being with God in nature? Can you start with the simple steps of going to the park, as I mentioned above? Why or why not?

Chapter 16

COURAGE: LEARNING TO CONQUER FEAR

BY DAVE

John Wayne is credited with saying, "Courage is being scared to death and saddling up anyway!" Many times during my journey, I have lacked courage and have suffered utter despair and humiliation. But I am not defeated. I am not a victim. I choose to refuse those labels.

What if Christ had refused the cross? What if Abraham had not been willing to sacrifice his son and missed God's blessing? What if Mary, Bathsheba, Ruth, Rahab, Tamar, or any other woman in Jesus's lineage had been aborted? Who would have saved us?

Listen to what God told the nation of Israel in Isaiah 43:1-4 as he speaks to them about fear:

But now, this is what the Lord says—
  he who created you, Jacob,
  he who formed you, Israel:
"Do not fear, for I have redeemed you;
  I have summoned you by name; you are mine.
When you pass through the waters,
  I will be with you;
and when you pass through the rivers,
  they will not sweep over you.
When you walk through the fire,
  you will not be burned;
  the flames will not set you ablaze.
For I am the Lord your God,
  the Holy One of Israel, your Savior;
I give Egypt for your ransom,
  Cush and Seba in your stead.
Since you are precious and honored in my sight,
  and because I love you,
I will give people in exchange for you,
  nations in exchange for your life.

The phrase "fear not" is stated over a hundred times in the Bible. Fear is a natural result of broken relationships and sin, and God wants to drive it away from us. American culture seems to breed fear into us through media, video games, movies, and other things we call "entertainment" or "enlightenment."

Life is hard, and it has always been hard. People all over the world lose jobs and loved ones. They experience pandemics. Everyone has bad days or suffers from people treating them wrong. All of us are misunderstood. And when we are misunderstood, we get into all kinds of messes with people we love and people we don't even know.

Paul gave a young pastor, Timothy, an encouraging word when he said, "For the Spirit God gave us does not make us timid, but gives us power, love, and self-discipline." (2 Timothy 1:7) How do we get past our fear and move into the power, love, and self-discipline Paul talks about? I've learned that it has to do with worship and humility. I become more humble by focusing on God and giving Him adoration, respect, reverence, and love. Worship helps my faith grow. My problems become smaller when I place them next to the Lord of all Creation.

Is it easy? No. In fact, the self-discipline of courage is what led me to write this book and tell my story. I was about to lose everything before I learned about taking action and having courage. I've had to look fear in the eye and develop courage in several different ways.

THE COURAGE TO FACE MY BRAIN INJURY

After my accident, I knew I was injured, but I did not acknowledge that my life was forever changed. To put it another way, I didn't realize how broken I was. It is not just a problem that I have; it is a problem we have as humans. We don't see our own brokenness, even when it's painfully obvious.

Today, I walk with a limp because my right ankle is fused. My left arm and hand are partially paralyzed, and I do not have much movement in either of them. I can do tasks that only need large motor skills, but I cannot do much that requires a soft touch or finesse.

Outwardly, I look fine except for walking with a limp. When I looked in the mirror, I saw a guy with a few problems but not a guy struggling to make sense of life. What I did not want to let myself realize, what I did not want to admit, is the permanently broken state of my brain.

On a traumatic brain injury chart, my brain damage is not just severe; it is even worse. There are three categories: mild, moderate, and severe. Mine is worse than severe.

If you look at the graph below, you'll see four categories of Traumatic Brain Injury (TBI): Mild, Moderate, and Severe. Mild TBI (mTBI) symptoms usually persist for about one month, and the brain returns to normal. Medium and Severe TBI injuries take longer to heal, with most of the healing occurring in the first year and very little, if any, healing occurring three years after the injury. Moderate and Severe TBI recovery varies based on the areas of the brain injured and the length of unconsciousness. Moderate TBI usually recovers around half of the previous brain capacity. Patients with Severe TBI often recover one-fourth of the capacity of the injured portions of the brain. [1]

Traumatic Brain Injury (TBI)			
Classification	**Length of Unconsciousness**	**Recovery Time**	**Recovery Capacity**
Mild (75-80% of cases)	Less than 30 minutes	About one month	Full brain function
Moderate (10-15% of cases)	30 minutes to 24 hours	Typically 1-3 years	Approx. ½ of previous capacity
Severe (10% of cases)	More than 24 hours	Typically 1-3 years	Approx ¼ of previous capacity

Severe TBI is defined by unconsciousness of greater than twenty-four hours and is normally measured in hours or a very few days. I was unconscious for one month—a full thirty days. I learned from my wife and friends that my brain was flowering, which is a nice way of saying it was bleeding like crazy the first week.

My neurologist recently explained things to me like this. My brain was slammed so hard into my skull that I have a closed skull brain injury called a diffuse axonal injury (DAI). I have sheared neurons and axions, brain cells and tissue that form nerves. The accident jarred my brain so hard that it permanently sheared nerve bundles and blood vessels in my brain. Not only is the brain injured, but the oxygen and nutrient supply needed to rebuild and restore the brain is damaged as well.

Parts of my brain are now dead after being cut off from the blood supply. But God's design for the human body is nothing short of amazing. My brain rerouted and made new information superhighways so that I could live. Orpha has let me know that from a professional's standpoint, I should be dead. Forget talking and having conversations with them—I should not be alive based on the levels of my brain injury. Honestly, I shouldn't be talking at all. I shouldn't remember anything.

THE COURAGE TO "OWN IT"

A few months before writing this book, I had to come to grips with where I am eight years after the accident. I had to face the reality that I will never go back to work. Not only am I not going back to work, but I am not the Dave I used to be.

I can't think, process, and understand things like I did before the accident. Maybe I was really smart before, and now my thinking is more average. I know that I cannot think like I used to. My emotions are permanently compromised. Good emotional control requires the ability to process events and information, then act upon them. I cannot process very well, so I react more from instinct than reason. The neuropathy in my body is also spreading. My limbs, which were already damaged, are becoming more numb and are losing movement because of the nerve damage. The burning sensations in my legs and feet sometimes become unbearable. It feels like my legs, up to the knees, are dangling in a vat of acid!

I got to a point where I was just done with life. I wanted it all to be over. I had to go and talk to people to change my thinking and to give me some hope. I spoke with my friend, Lance (you'll hear more about him in a bit), my pastor, and others. I had to accept where I am and say to myself, "I am done being done." I chose to live and make a new life.

As soon as I got to that point where I was "done being done," I accepted myself and my life. I started to figure out how to deal with who I am and what I can do today. I knew I could not rely on drugs for the rest of my life because, after eight years, they are losing their positive effects. I did not want to take opioids and other drugs to manage pain and deal with a great amount of mental fog for the rest of my life.

I had to take over my own medical care with alternative therapies and find what works for me and my broken body. The hard work is paying dividends. I now use a hyperbaric chamber to flood my body with pressurized oxygen. It feeds my body, especially my brain. Neuropathy devices and rebuilder nerve stimulators help the nerves of my feet and legs. These types of treatments are not normal in western medicine.

As of the writing of this book, I'm just a few weeks into these new treatments. If these few weeks are any indication of what is possible, I will be fixed up much better than where I am now. Like I said, my legs were full of pain. Now the burning only comes from time to time, and sometimes, they're pain free!

I've had to give up cigars to keep my legs from burning. Even though I don't inhale the smoke (at least not on purpose), it's enough to slow down my circulation and cause the neuropathy to flare. So, I had to let go of cigars. Thank God I stopped drinking. Without a good understanding of what it meant to be sober before I got hurt, it would have been easy to pick up the bottle and go back to drinking after the coma.

My speech is improving. I am not the best judge, but others notice that I am speaking more clearly, and my cadence is faster. Thanks to super infusions of oxygen twice a day, five times a week,

I can think faster. Right now, I'm taking it one day at a time. I have a good plan to kick this pain to the curb and fix my brain from its current state of disarray.

The first step was "owning it." I needed to own who I am, my condition, and my reality. Second, I had to take responsibility for my state and take responsibility for making changes. Third, I had to figure out a plan and then do it.

THE COURAGE TO SOLVE PROBLEMS

I find this all ironic. Problem-solving was second nature for me as the VP of Plant Operations. Figuring out problems was a big part of my work. I used to sit in the back of the room and watch my team run through the problem-solving process and go through the different steps to arrive at a good solution.

Those steps involved identifying and naming a problem so that everyone shared a clear focus, defining the measurement of the problem, and using other tools to get to the root cause of the problem. Now, I need to run through the same problem-solving process on myself!

One day, I called Orpha in and said, "Sit down, and let me show you what I've been doing." She didn't care about the particular pieces and exactly what I was doing. She was happy that I was taking control of my health and my life again.

I was done being done, and I wanted to prove it to myself and my wife. And I did! I used the tools that Deryl, the guy from Toyota, taught us for problem-solving in order to solve myself. I was the problem that I needed to solve. I did not need to solve anyone else. No other person could solve my problems, no matter how much they loved, cared for, or knew me.

When you stop looking to do something else and stop looking for someone to come and save you, that's when you know you are "done being done."

My current steps for taking control of my health are the hyperbaric chamber visits and a new team to deal with the neuropathy in Boise. They are all busy, and I have several health-related irons in the fire with a new team helping me make my brain the best it can be. We all know my treatment will never return my brain to its original state of health, but we can make it better together.

WHAT I LEARNED FROM LANCE MCCULLOUGH

Lance McCullough is a mighty man of God and an amazing human being. Lance's background as a contractor and his love for the Lord, made him the perfect guy to lead mission trips for our church. I must have gone on twelve to fifteen trips with Lance to build churches, clinics, and schools in Latin and South America. Lance led my first mission trip experience when I went to Belize.

Lance is married with two daughters and a son. From what I've mentioned, you probably think he lives a completely normal life. But you'd be wrong. Lance has ALS, Amyotrophic Lateral Sclerosis, otherwise known as Lou Gehrig's disease. ALS is a progressive disease that destroys nerve cells controlling voluntary muscle movement.

During the last few trips I made with Lance and the church to Central America, we brought his motorized scooter. Special permission was necessary to haul it on the airplane and get it through border control and customs.

Lance was diagnosed with ALS around fifteen years ago but has refused to let it slow him down. His symptoms started with the loss of feeling and control in his legs, and it continued to move upward from there. Where the symptoms began to manifest is part of the miracle of why he is still alive. Most people have a life expectancy of three to four years after they receive their ALS diagnosis.

Lance has been part of his own long-life miracle. He is an incredibly faithful man to God and others. He finds ways to share the message and love of Jesus from his wheelchair. Lance had to close his company, so he began to focus on impacting young lives as a volunteer football coach at two local high schools in Bakersfield, California. He did all that from his special wheelchair, rolling up and down sidelines and worksites.

Lance was an incredible athlete selected to represent Team USA in the 1984 Olympics in Los Angeles. But instead of chasing a gold medal, he married his high school sweetheart, and they began building their life together. He started and operated McCullough Construction. Lance ran his business like he runs the rest of his life. The company is straightforward, delivers what it promises, and stands behind all its work.

I appreciate and fear this trait of Lance; he will always tell me the truth. If something is bothering me and I call him, he will tell me if I am the problem, if it is a bad situation, or if it is an attack from the evil one. He'll tell me not to let the devil get a foothold in my mind, no matter the situation. I know that is why I've hesitated to speak with him at times. He's a truth-teller. But I always feel better after I speak with him.

I can't tell you how many lives Lance has impacted or still is impacting. How many guys get out and coach kids from a wheelchair while they are battling ALS? He's such a courageous man. Simply by living his life, encouraging others, and being a truth-teller, he instills courage into others around him.

ALS is a merciless killer that slowly destroys the body, leaving the mind and soul of the patient fully intact. Lance recommends watching the Amazon documentary "Gleason," which follows former New Orleans Saints defensive back and local hero Steve Gleason's battle with ALS. The documentary shows how the body of a top athlete falls apart and challenges him—not to mention his wife as a caregiver.

Lance is still Lance, and his mind is fully working. He's becoming more and more of a mind and spirit trapped in a body that keeps losing function. For a long time, Lance fought the advancing disease and used leg braces and special crutches to keep moving. Moving was hard, and he pushed for as long as he could, fighting to keep his mobility until his body lost its ability to stand and move under its own power.

He had a device implanted to help his diaphragm continue to lift his lungs so he could breathe. But he vowed never to get a tracheotomy or be hooked up to a breathing machine like Stephen Hawking. Lance does not want to put his wife through that kind of experience and decision-making later on. I don't know if he has changed his mind on that, but I do know a few things about Lance.

Lance McCullough is one heck of a soul. He continues to fight for life and encourage others with a decaying body. It's hard to watch. It is hard to see a good friend meet his maker in such a prolonged death.

Lance's wife, Leeta, has help and support as a caretaker. A young man who has been close to them over the years lives with them. He is Lance's primary support. Lance can't feed himself anymore, so he's there to help Lance eat. Lance still loves sushi and is still able to go out and enjoy eating with family and friends. God provided well for all of them by drawing them close together. The young man has always called Lance and his wife "mom and dad." They are special people.

I find it hard to watch a man struggle but make no mistake, Lance McCullough is not reduced by ALS. Yes, he is hobbled, and he cannot lift a spoon to feed himself, but he is a giant of a man. He has a giant soul with faith that moves mountains. He loves people and believes in them. He loves the Lord, and rather than shrinking and being reduced; he continues to grow in favor in the sight of God and man. Nothing will ever rob him of his identity in Jesus Christ. We saw him bring God's kingdom here on earth through sacrificial ministry, and he is still speaking truth.

Lance has taught me more about courage than any other person. All of us have to weather changes in life, and I have seen Lance make massive changes in stride better than I can imagine any other person.

A few months before I decided to be "done being done," I hit my lowest low. I kept thinking, "I'm done with this life. I am tired and want to be done with hurting all the time. I'm done, and I want to go away. I do not want to be in this body or life anymore."

So, I called Lance. We talked for an hour on the phone, and everything changed. My life did a complete one-eighty. I started our conversation by saying, "I'm done," meaning I have no more will to fight. By the end of the conversation, I started saying, "I'm done being done!" Why? Because I spoke with Lance McCullough.

Lance can't do anything for himself anymore. If the dog jumps on his lap and scratches him, he feels it but can't swat the dog away. He can't move to change his position. Lance, a guy who cannot do anything for himself, shared three things with me that changed the trajectory of my life.

1. Be done being done.
2. Ask for help.
3. Have faith beyond all measure.

That conversation with Lance got me into "solving myself." It helped me see that I could use my problem-solving skills to not only help others but to help myself as well. I did not give up. I found new ways to get help. I started believing more in God, His grace, the love of my family, and myself.

A FEW IDEAS FOR BECOMING MORE COURAGEOUS

When I consider what it means to be courageous, I can't help but think of the beginning of the book of Joshua:

After the death of Moses the servant of the Lord, the Lord said to Joshua son of Nun, Moses' aide: "Moses my servant is dead. Now then, you and all these people, get ready to cross the Jordan River into the land I am about to give to them—to the Israelites. I will give you every place where you set your foot, as I promised Moses. Your territory will extend from the desert to Lebanon, and from the great river, the Euphrates—all the Hittite country—to the Mediterranean Sea in the west. No one will be able to stand against you all the days of your life. As I was with Moses, so I will be with you; I will never leave you nor forsake you. Be strong and courageous, because you will lead these people to inherit the land I swore to their ancestors to give them.

"Be strong and very courageous. Be careful to obey all the law my servant Moses gave you; do not turn from it to the right or to the left, that you may be successful wherever you go. Keep this Book of the Law always on your lips; meditate on it day and night, so that you may be careful to do everything written in it. Then you will be prosperous and successful. Have I not commanded you? Be strong and courageous. Do not be afraid; do not be discouraged, for the Lord your God will be with you wherever you go."

— Joshua 1:1-9

God commanded Joshua to be courageous. God was not making a suggestion or a polite request. No, God commanded the man leading God's children to have courage.

Joshua and Caleb were the oldest men in all of Israel and the only two men who had seen all the ten plagues in Egypt, the crossing of the Red Sea, the incredible bounty of the Promised Land, and all the other works and miracles God worked through Moses. So, you could say Joshua had a lot of reasons to have courage and faith in God.

Why, then, was God commanding him to "be strong and courageous?" Joshua had proven himself courageous enough to stand up against popular opinion and ridicule when the other spies sent into the promised land cowered in the face of giants.

Taking responsibility for your life and for leading others requires a different type of courage than planning, thinking, or reading. Joshua's new responsibility as a leader meant he had to take action rooted in the character and nature of God. He was acting as God's leader, not just a follower.

Jesus calls all of us to the same kind of life. We are commanded to be "salt and light" in the world. We are responsible for living a life of action rooted in God's word and steeped in his love.

That's what Lance McCullough was teaching me that day on the phone. It changed my life.

The good news for Joshua, and all of us, is that God does not just give us loose and vague instructions for a courageous life. No, it starts with being steeped and rooted in the Word of God. But there are also some practical things we can do to become more courageous. Here are a few that work for me.

Stop watching the news. Turn off the stuff that brings you down and naturally gets you angry. Stop putting yourself in front of people who put you in a bad mood and make you a darker person.

Pray and really talk to God. Talk to him as a friend. You do not need some special prayer where you just sit in a certain corner at home or at church. Just say a simple prayer wherever you are, such as, "Lord, here I am. I want to talk to you about something." Just share what you have to share with him. There's no special formula. If it helps and you don't know what to say, start with a Psalm or the Lord's Prayer and then just talk to God like He's a friend.

Surround yourself with courageous people. When you spend time with courageous people, you can't help but be courageous yourself. Their power comes from their positivity and their good nature. Put yourself in the middle of strong, resilient people and let them help you.

You can support them, but you have to let the people you trust, support and help you as well. They are your foundation for greater things.

Get out with your family and friends. When I take my kids out, they fill up my soul. Go to a park, a movie, or get candy or ice cream with your kids. Spend time without expectations. They will fill your soul.

I can't speak for you, but there is a lot at stake for me to be and remain courageous. My emotional problems were getting the best of me, and I was losing my family. I couldn't be around my kids without losing my temper. I couldn't be around my wife without taking out my pain and frustrations on her.

That was the hardest part of my accident, and coming to grips with myself. I couldn't stand the person I had become. I knew that is not who I was, who I am, or who I wanted to be. So, I had to get courageous and choose to live.

I thought getting sober was hard, but this change in life is the hardest thing I've ever done. Here is the good news, though; the hardest things in life are also the most valuable. Trust me; it's worth it. It's worth it to be courageous and face the challenges in front of you. With God at your side, powering you with strength and wisdom, you can face anything.

One final thought as we close this chapter (and this book). Maybe you're reading this and thinking, "I wish I could be like Joshua. I wish I could be courageous under difficult circumstances." Remember, your courage doesn't come from inside yourself. It comes from God and the power He gives you. If you're not feeling courageous, ask Him for strength, wisdom, and bravery. Just like a tree needs the resistance of the wind to make it stronger and taller, we all need difficulties to make us stronger in courage and faith.

When we realize our weaknesses and open ourselves up to all the wonderful things God has in store for us, we can truly experience God Shots.

GOD SHOTS FOR SUCCESS

1. Life is messy. Our greatest problems are not with the messes that land on us or happen to us, but with the messed-up thinking, attitudes, and actions we have inside. What fears are holding you back from being who God wants you to be right now?

2. How is God showing you to be "done being done?" Is there an area of your life where you need to pick up more responsibility and begin living more fully? On the outside, we might look "fine," "okay," or "not bad," and inside, be full of despair. Take an honest inventory.

3. I'm so thankful God put Lance McCullough into my life. I don't know where I would be without his wisdom, prayers, and example. Who is your "Lance?" Have you spoken with that person lately? If so, what did they tell you? Did you take their advice seriously and put it into practice?

4. Lance changed my life with three insights. Which one of these do you need to work on right now? 1) Be done being done. 2) Ask for help. 3) Have faith beyond all measure.

5. Review the practical ideas that work for me above. Which one can you use to help you take courage? Is there a practical thing that you know God wants you to do to become more courageous, but instead, you choose fear? What is it?

Appendix A

GETTING HELP FOR ALCOHOLISM

n Chapter 6, I gave you a peek behind the curtain of my addiction to alcohol. In this Appendix, I want to go deeper and give you straight talk about how to get help for this very serious problem.

If this is a struggle for you, I want to begin by telling you that AA (Alcoholics Anonymous) is one of the best self-help programs around, if not *the* best around. First, just find out where the closest AA meetings are. Go introduce yourself as a new guy. If you don't want to say you are an alcoholic, don't say you're an alcoholic. Just say, "Hi, I'm so-and-so; I'm a new guy."

The people in the meeting will not judge you. Just put your hand out and meet people. That's it. That's what it takes to get started.

I guarantee that if you walk into an AA meeting, the people there have done more bad stuff than you could ever think of doing. I have heard some of the biggest, craziest stories in AA meetings. I've heard of drunk people stealing fighter jets and flying them across the country! I've heard people say, "Oh, yeah, I once got drunk, and I got married in Vegas!"

There are very few problems that can compete with that. You think your problems are the end all be all, but I can guarantee there's someone in the room who will almost always have worse problems than you. Don't let your problems keep you from going to a meeting.

At the end of the day, when you put all the problems on the table, you will find that your problems are not as bad as you thought, and you'll gladly take them back. Even small towns, such like where I live have AA meetings twice a week. Places with more people, like where I used to live, have meetings seven days a week.

Whenever you feel like drinking, just pick up the phone or show up at a meeting. It's that simple. I know a guy from California who worked in Eastern Europe. The culture there is centered on alcohol. They drink vodka like water! He found AA meetings over there. He couldn't understand the language, but he went anyway.

No matter where you are in the world, the meetings are the same. Whether you're on a cruise ship, a hotel, or a casino in Vegas, AA meetings are happening. Just say, "I'm a friend of Bill W.," one of AA's founders, and people will point you to a meeting.

I used to lie to myself and say, "You know what? I'm going to change. I'm gonna get a support guy. I will get Kevin Kelly, a guy from church, to help me." That was a lie. I had no intention of telling a friend or someone who could have been my friend the truth about me. When you walk into an AA meeting, you will meet folks who are just like you. You will feel at home. It's an awesome fellowship.

So, if AA is so great, why do so many Christians avoid it even though they know it could help them? Here is the reason; a lot of people in the church believe Jesus came to save the clean. He didn't come to help healthy people; He came to heal and help those who needed it. He came for the sick and wounded.

When you walk into a church, too many people there think it has to be full of "clean and whole" people just like them. When I talk about how the church needs to be filled with the broken and messed up, some people's reactions make me sick. I know the church is a house of prayer, but at the same time, it is also a house of ill repute.

Why? It's simple; it's a house for people like me . . . and you.

I still see myself as a drunk sometimes, even though I'm a sober alcoholic. I know I could go back to it at any moment. But we do not go to church until we get "fixed" and figure out life first. That's backward!

Go to church until you get yourself straight. Go to church until you get over your addiction. Go to church until you figure out your path. But don't figure out your path and then go to church.

I can tell you AA was founded and is grounded in Christianity. In AA, we say you need to believe in a "higher power" and do not define it for people. That's fine, but at some point, you have to realize the higher power is Jesus.

Go to https://aa.org to find a meeting near you, or call the AA office in your neck of the woods. There are meetings in some amazing places. Ask the front desk at a hotel in Vegas. Or ask them if anyone knows Bill Wilson (an AA founder). You'd be surprised.

Until you get healing, get yourself in the middle of the herd. Get yourself in church. You don't have to be clean as a whistle. Just go and hear the Word and be close to God. Of course, you don't have to go to church to join AA; just be willing . . . willing to quit drinking!

A LETTER TO SARAH ANNE

E arlier in the book, I mentioned that we lost our precious daughter, Sarah Anne. Shortly after she left us, I wrote a eulogy for her I'd like to share with you here.

God blessed us with you, Sarah Anne. I say that He blessed us because He could have given you to anyone, and He chose us. He trusted us with you, a precious little Angel! You weren't supposed to be with us for more than a moment, but you stayed. You stayed to fulfill something much greater than we'll ever understand until we get to see you again!

Maybe it was for your mommy and me. That's probably a little selfish on our part, though.

Maybe it was to touch the lives of those who met you, loved you, or will hear your story.

Maybe it was to teach us how precious a moment truly is and how we all take them for granted. How quickly one flashes by, but how great the love you can fill it with. You showed us that, Sarah.

Maybe it was to show folks the power of prayer. There were so many praying for you and us.

Maybe it was to remind us that miracles do happen! Miracles are so easy to miss in today's world. But you showed us so many. Two minutes turned to twenty minutes. Then it turned to hours, then to days. We got four days! Four amazing days.

We got to hold you, sing with you, pray with you. I especially liked our special version of the Shepherd's Prayer and our "night night" prayers. We cuddled you; we kissed you; we got to hold your hands. We walked in the afternoon sunlight outside. None of the other babies got to do that!

The other day, I tried to count the number of times we sang "You Are My Sunshine." I have to be honest—I wish for one more. Your mommy would cuddle you for what seemed like forever, gently stroking your forehead and whispering to you late at night. Neither of us could sleep a wink, especially your mommy, for fear of missing a single moment with you.

Sarah, we miss you so much it hurts. But don't worry about your mommy and me, your sister Paige, or now your brother David. God is taking care of us, but you already know that. No one is promised in this life no pain, no sadness, no suffering—only comfort and a way through if we ask and have faith. Even in times of despair and sadness, God cradles us all in his hands, and Jesus walks with us . . . when He's not carrying us.

Thursday night, on my way home from the store, you spoke to me, Sarah. You said, "I'm okay, Daddy." Thank you! That made me feel lots better, little Angel.

We love and miss you and can't wait to see you again.

ACKNOWLEDGMENTS

First, I would like to thank my late father, Richard Charles Blanchat. Thank you for becoming a grandfather that your grandchildren were happy to know and play with and a father I will miss in this life. Love, your son.

To my mother, Mary Lynn Blanchat, thank you for all your help while I was in a coma and after. Thank you. Your help meant the world to Orpha and me when we needed it most. We love you.

I would also like to thank Mr. Lance McCullough, truly a man of God who has been living with ALS. Thank you for your love and infinite wisdom—first, as my lead on numerous mission trips to Central and South America, and then as a true friend who helped me navigate my "new life." Thank you.

And to Orval, my brother-in-law. Thank you for almost losing your job, not only for me but for your sister. You carried her when she needed support, wisdom . . . and Dr. Google!

Thank you to Kent Sanders for helping us organize and craft our story so we could share it with the world.

Thank you, Will Matthews, for your coaching and insight. Be blessed, brutha!

And to all my friends at Paramount Farms, Inc., Wonderful Pistachios and Almonds, thank you! Whether a past employee, coworker, or anyone working with me and praying for me, thank you! Your continued prayers made the difference. I am forever in your debt. Gracias mis amigos.

ABOUT THE AUTHORS

Dave and Orpha Blanchat are Christians who believe in having Faith over Fear. They live in Idaho with their two children, Paige and David. They have been married for thirty-two years and are both motivational speakers.

Dave graduated from Oregon State University with a BS in Industrial and Manufacturing Engineering in 1991. He is an avid fly fisherman and outdoor enthusiast. Dave has attended fifteen overseas mission trips to Central and South America. He retired as VP of Operations from Paramount Farms, Inc./Wonderful after a catastrophic auto accident in 2014.

Orpha is a Life Coach, inspirational speaker, writer, and Former Ministry Leader of The Battleground of Purity and the Couples Hands Ministry. She is also the Former Director of the Bakersfield Pregnancy Center. Orpha is an avid kayaker and loves shopping at antique stores.

You can find out more about Dave and Orpha's story at https://www.god-shots.com, on Instagram at godshots_ourstory, or reach them directly via email at

daveandorpha@god-shots.com.

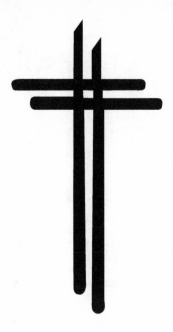

ENDNOTES

1   The information in the chart below is adapted from https://verdugopsych.com/neuropsychological-evaluation-of-traumatic-brain-injury/.

A free ebook edition is available with the purchase of this book.

To claim your free ebook edition:

1. Visit MorganJamesBOGO.com
2. Sign your name CLEARLY in the space
3. Complete the form and submit a photo of the entire copyright page
4. You or your friend can download the ebook to your preferred device

Morgan James
BOGO™

A **FREE** ebook edition is available for you
or a friend with the purchase of this print book.

CLEARLY SIGN YOUR NAME ABOVE

Instructions to claim your free ebook edition:
1. Visit MorganJamesBOGO.com
2. Sign your name CLEARLY in the space above
3. Complete the form and submit a photo
   of this entire page
4. You or your friend can download the ebook
   to your preferred device

Print & Digital Together Forever.

Snap a photo   Free ebook   Read anywhere